Students an... E...

LONDON
200 YEARS AGO
by
W. Crawford Snowden

PROFUSELY ILLUSTRATED WITH PHOTOGRAPHS, OLD PRINTS AND MAP SECTIONS — PRICE 7/6

LONDON
200 YEARS AGO

by W. Crawford Snowden

WITH AN INTRODUCTION BY

E. G. R. Taylor
D.SC., F.R.G.S., F.R.HIST.SOC.

Temple Barr.

THE "DAILY MAIL" SERVES EDUCATION

Pit Ticket

WILLIAM HOGARTH, great painter and pictorial satirist, was fifty at the time of our map. He liked to regard himself as author rather than artist, and, as Lamb so aptly says, " His graphic representations are indeed books ; they have the teeming, fruitful suggestiveness of words." He has been called " writer of comedy with a pencil," and " graphic moralist."

" The Cockpit," engraved in 1759, was one of William Hogarth's last paintings. The scene is the Cock Pit on the south side of St. James's Park, demolished in 1816 : Cockpit Steps, in Dartmouth Street, marks the site. Jockeys and cock-breeders, sweeps and Quakers, English dukes and French marquises, blind men and deaf men, are absorbed in the exciting " sport " and greed of easy gain. Many of those depicted were well-known characters of the time.

The reflection on the table is the shadow of a man who has been drawn up to the ceiling in a basket. This was a punishment in cockpit law, for making bets for more money than one could pay. The culprit's shadow is fruitlessly tendering his watch to satisfy his creditors.

CONTENTS

PICTURES

Typical of the Year 1746

Top picture shows an early eighteenth-century drawing-room with carved pine panelling. This was originally at No. 27 Hatton Garden, then a high-class residential district. The dress is similar to that worn by people of distinction visiting Ranelagh. The shoe and clog are in silk and brocade.

Photographs by courtesy of the Victoria and Albert Museum.

JOHN ROCQUE AND HIS MAPS

JOHN ROCQUE, like so many able professional men in Hanoverian England, was of Huguenot extraction, coming of a family of French small landowners. Trained as a draughtsman, his earliest occupation, dating from 1734, was drawing plans, prospects, and elevations of the great country mansions, the " gentlemen's seats " as they were called, which, set in their formal gardens, were one of the landscape beauties of the period.

His talent must have attracted attention, for two engravers named Pine and Tinney, who themselves also made topographical drawings, engaged him to make a survey of London at their expense. This work, the fine map here reproduced, he commenced in 1737, but it was nine years before the resulting drawing which Pine himself engraved was actually ready for publication.

Meanwhile Rocque commenced a fresh survey of the capital to include the surrounding countryside, and after securing a list of subscribers himself published this second great map which he had engraved by Richard Parr. Both maps appeared in 1746, and perhaps there was some ill-feeling, for when after another nine years had elapsed the Pine and Tinney map was revised and re-engraved " with all the new roads that have been made on account of Westminster Bridge," the two men announced that together with Thomas Bowles (a well-

known print-seller) they were proprietors of the original survey by Rocque.

John Rocque's own latest revision seems to have been in 1761, just before his death, by which date he was able to describe himself as " Topographer (or alternatively ' Chorographer ') to His Majesty."

In the course of nearly thirty years he had built up an important business on premises near Hyde Park Corner as land-surveyor, engraver and general map-seller which his widow Mary Ann continued to carry on with the help of the old employees for another ten years or so.

Apart from his survey maps of London and district, issued in numerous styles, Rocque's most important contribution to geography was his four large-scale county maps, Shropshire, Middlesex, Berkshire, and Surrey, which are unique as the first " land-use " maps, for they show, besides all the detailed topography, the arable, pasture and rough grassland areas. All were made from his own surveys carried out between 1752 and 1761, and it was perhaps while he was making a plan of Shrewsbury in 1746 that the idea was first suggested to Rocque of embarking upon the whole county of Shropshire, the first actual county he undertook.

Anyone who compares Rocque's maps and plans with their modern counterparts will find them remarkably

The method by which topographers made their measurements is illustrated in this Hyde Park Corner scene from an eighteenth-century map by Joshua Rhodes. The topographer wheels his old-type perambulator along to record accurately the length of each street. The circumference of the perambulator was 8 ft. 3 ins.

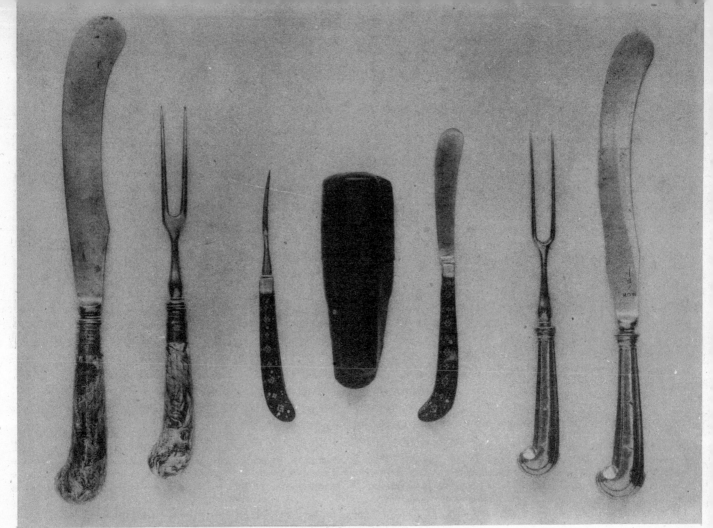

English knives and forks, eighteenth-century.

Photograph by courtesy of the Victoria and Albert Museum.

Two wine bottles, 1740-1745. Bottles at this period were just beginning to approach modern form.

An eighteenth-century wooden printing press of about 1750.

Photographs by courtesy of the London Museum.

THE IMPORTS OF GREAT BRITAIN FROM FRANCE
A mid-eighteenth-century engraving

The artist, L. P. Boitard, gives this explanation :—Four tackle porters staggering under a weighty chest. Behind, several emaciated high-lived epicures familiarly receiving a French cook. . . . A lady of distinction offering the tuition of her son and daughter to a cringing French Abbe. A woman of quality greeting a French female dancer.

The barrels and cases in the foreground contain French cheeses from Normandy, Tippets, Muffs, Ribands, Flowers for the hair, Beauty Washes, Perfumes, Gloves, French wines and brandies. At a distance landing, swarms of Milliners, Taylors, Frisers, Tutoresses for Boarding Schools, Distinguished Jesuits, Quacks, etc., etc.

By courtesy of the Library Committee of the Corporation of London.

accurate, for by his day instrumental survey, with perambulator, plane-table and theodolite was already nearly two centuries old. The first modern land-surveyor of whom we have any certain knowledge was Ralph Agas, a Suffolk man, who also made the first " modern " map of London in 1560 (although there is some controversy about this date).

This map is best known by an engraving of much later date (1748) made by Rocque's contemporary Vertue. Agas was followed by John Norden, surveyor alike of estates, cities and counties. His map of London (1593) was copied and revised again and again during the first half of the seventeenth century for it was used to illustrate the guide-books printed for visitors up from the country.

Then came the Great Fire which put all former maps out of date. The Lord Mayor immediately set eight of the most notable surveyors of the day to work upon drawing a street plan on which to base the re-building of the City, but a much more popular and saleable publication was the engraving showing twin prospects— London before and after the Fire. This was the work of Wenceslaus Hollar, a Czech artist settled in this country, who had also engraved the official street plan.

Rebuilding was rapid, and by 1677 the new London

was worthily re-mapped by John Ogilby, maker of the famous first road books of England and Wales, who was assisted by his young kinsman William Morgan. Ogilby himself was not a surveyor, he had been a dancing-master and organiser of plays and revels, but his losses in the Fire caused him to turn to the production of books and maps, using the best professional men he could find, including Hollar. He died just before his map of London was issued, but Morgan was appointed Cosmographer Royal in his stead, and although hampered by lack of capital was able to bring out a second large-scale map, covering both London and Westminster, in 1682.

During the next fifty years or so the map-sellers produced plenty of maps of London which they claimed as new and up to date, but none of these has any particular importance or interest. It was left to John Rocque to perambulate the streets once more and to set out the plot of Georgian London as Ogilby and Morgan had depicted London after the Interregnum and as Norden and Agas had put on record the very much smaller London of Queen Elizabeth.

E. G. R. TAYLOR, D.Sc.,
F.R.G.S., F.R.HIST.SOC.,
Emeritus Professor of Geography in the University of London

Fireplace and overmantel of pinewood about 1750-1760. Removed
from No. 5 Great George Street, London, W.9 in 1910.

Photograph by courtesy of the Victoria and Albert Museum

THE FOUNDLING HOSPITAL

The South view of the hospital that has been described as "the most useful among the numerous charities that are an honour to this age and nation," and, right, its founder Captain Thomas Coram. In circle, Handel, the great composer, a Foundling Hospital benefactor who "enriched the foundation by a new revenue raised from the powers of harmony, and has performed a sacred oratorio, playing the organ gratis." See Section C.1

Gentleman's Magazine,

AND

Historical Chronicle.

VOLUME XVI.

For the YEAR M.DCC.XLVI.

PRODESSE & DELECTARE.   E PLURIBUS UNUM.

By SYLVANUS URBAN Gent.

NEWS
IN
1746

"The Gentleman's Magazine," earliest literary journal of its kind, was flourishing at the time of our map, under its founder and first editor, Edward Cave. Its main purpose was to present the month's news in condensed form.

Cave began as a printer's apprentice, eventually set up a small press of his own, and in 1731 started the magazine at St. John's Gate, Clerkenwell. Dr. Johnson became its parliamentary reporter in 1740. They were fast friends, and Cave's hand was in Johnson's on January 10, 1754, when Cave died.

THE

Gentleman's Magazine,

For AUGUST, 1746.

A particular account of the manner of the execution of the earl of Kilmarnock and lord Balmerino, on the 18th inst. their behaviour, &c.

AT 6 o'clock a troop of life-guards, one of horse-gre-nadiers, and 1000 of the foot-guards (being fifteen men out of each company) marched from the parade in St James's park thro' the city to Tower-hill, to attend the execution of the earl of Kilmarnock and the lord Balmerino, and being arrived there were posted in lines from the Tower to the scaffold, and all round it. About 8 o'clock the sheriffs of London, with their under sheriffs and their officers, viz.

to the outward gate of the Tower, and after knocking at it some time, a warder within asked, who's there? the officer without replied, the sheriffs of London and Middlesex. The warder then asked, what do they want? the officer answered, the bodies of William earl of Kilmarnock, and Arthur lord Balmerino; upon which the warder within said, I will go and inform the lieutenant of the Tower, and in about 10 minutes the lieut. of the Tower with the earl of Kilmarnock,† and major White with lord Balmerino, guarded by several of the warders, came to the gate; the prisoners were there delivered to the sheriffs, who gave proper receipts for their bodies to the lieutenant, who, as is u-sual, said, God bless KING GEORGE; to which the earl of Kilmarnock assented by a bow, and the lord Balmerino said, God

10

THE MAP OF LONDON BY JOHN ROCQUE

Key Plan to the Map Sections

A contracted Sketch of the PLAN of LONDON &c. printed on 24 Sheets of Imperial Paper, to shew the General Appearance of the Whole; for the Use of those who bind it in a Book, and for the better comprehending the Divisions mentioned in the Index.

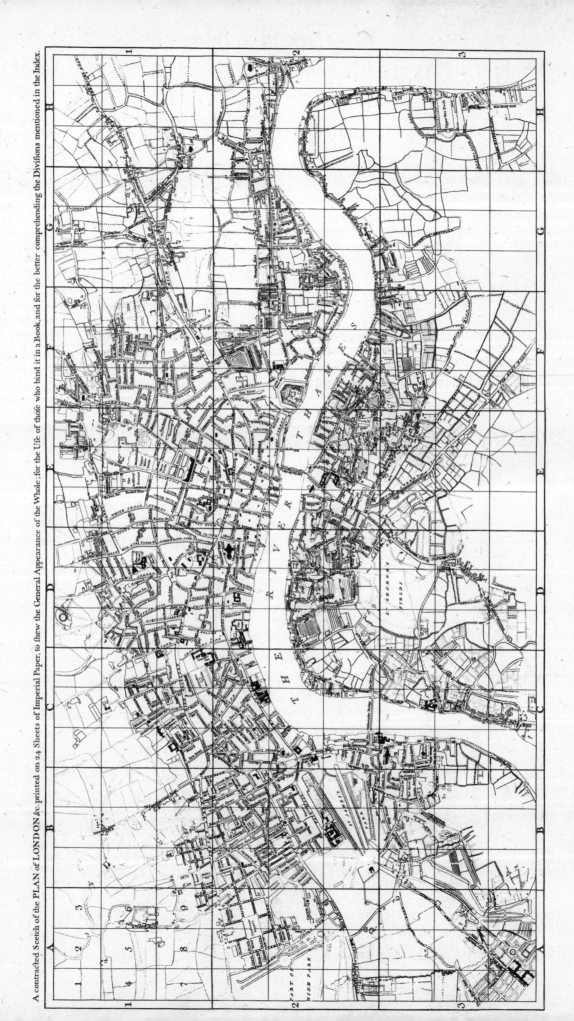

For easy reference this map has been divided into twenty-four sections. Horizontally, reading from left to right (A to H), and vertically from 1 to 3, the sections are reproduced in the following pages. Explanatory matter, historical and topographical, faces each section.

ADVENTURE IN MARYLEBONE FIELDS

TO place this north-west Section of our map in its corresponding position in modern London, let us look at the bottom of it for " Marybone " Lane. It is a turning out of Oxford Street you probably know. Follow it on our map to the village of St. Mary Le Bone, with Marybone Gardens on the right : Devonshire Street, off the present Marylebone High Street, and Beaumont Street which crosses it at right angles, are now on the site of Marybone Gardens.

Continue the same road north, and you come to Love Lane, in which the only building shown is Jews' Harp House. This famous tavern and tea gardens stood between the present Broad Walk of Regent's Park and the north-west side of the Botanic Gardens within the Park. That being so, one imagines the Zoological Gardens would be somewhere to the left of the letter (A) beyond the border of our map.

Marybone Gardens was a well-known place of entertainment when our map was drawn. It was surrounded by a brick wall set with fruit trees and had, as you can see, a circular walk. This was six paces wide and 485 paces round, " double set with quick-set hedges kept in excellent order, and indented like town walls." In the centre was a bowling green " 112 paces one way, 88 the other," much used by persons of quality.

Such was the condition of the roads round London that in 1746 the lessee of these gardens engaged " a guard of soldiers " to protect visitors to and from London, and a later lessee, in 1760, offered ten guineas reward for the apprehension of " any highwaymen found on the road to the Gardens." It was, of course, the scene of operations of Captain Macheath and his gang in *The Beggar's Opera*. The Gardens were in being until 1778.

Marybone Fields were often the rendezvous for duels. There is an amusing account of one fought in 1760, in which the Duke of Bolton " overreached himself, fell down and hurt his knee ; Mr. Stewart, his opponent, bid him get up, but

he could not : then he bid him ask for his life, but he would not : so he let him alone, and that's all."

Jews' Harp House appears to have been eminently respectable, for it was a favourite resort of the Speaker of the House of Commons, Mr. Speaker Onslow, who served five Parliaments, was Speaker for 33 years, and was renowned for his integrity. A description of the tavern written 27 years after our map was made says it consisted of a large upper room, ascended by a large outside staircase, for the accommodation of the company on ball nights, and in this room large parties dined.

" At the south front of these premises was a large enclosure, with boxes for tea and ale drinkers guarded by deal-board soldiers between every box, painted in proper colours. In the centre of this opening were tables and seats placed for the smokers. On the eastern side of the house there was a trap-ball ground (an early form of cricket) ; the western side served for a tennis-hall (real tennis) ; there were also public and private skittle grounds."

In the right-hand corner of this Section of our map is a small group of streets the names of which will be familiar. They are on the west side of Cavendish Square, and were laid out in 1717. But the further development of the West End at this point had ceased through the collapse in 1720 of the South Sea Company, when so many speculative schemes fell through.

The streets are named after relatives and possessions of the landowner, Edward Harley, second Earl of Oxford and Mortimer, son of the founder of the Harleian Collection of books and manuscripts in the British Museum. Thus Henrietta, daughter and heiress of John Holles, Duke of Newcastle, was his wife ; Elizabeth Vere was her mother ; Wimpole in Cambridgeshire was owned by Harley ; Wigmore Castle, Herefordshire, was the seat of the Mortimer family. Welbeck Street recalls Welbeck in Nottinghamshire, ancient seat of the Cavendish family, later that of the Dukes of Portland.

THE GRAND WALK, MARYLEBONE GARDENS

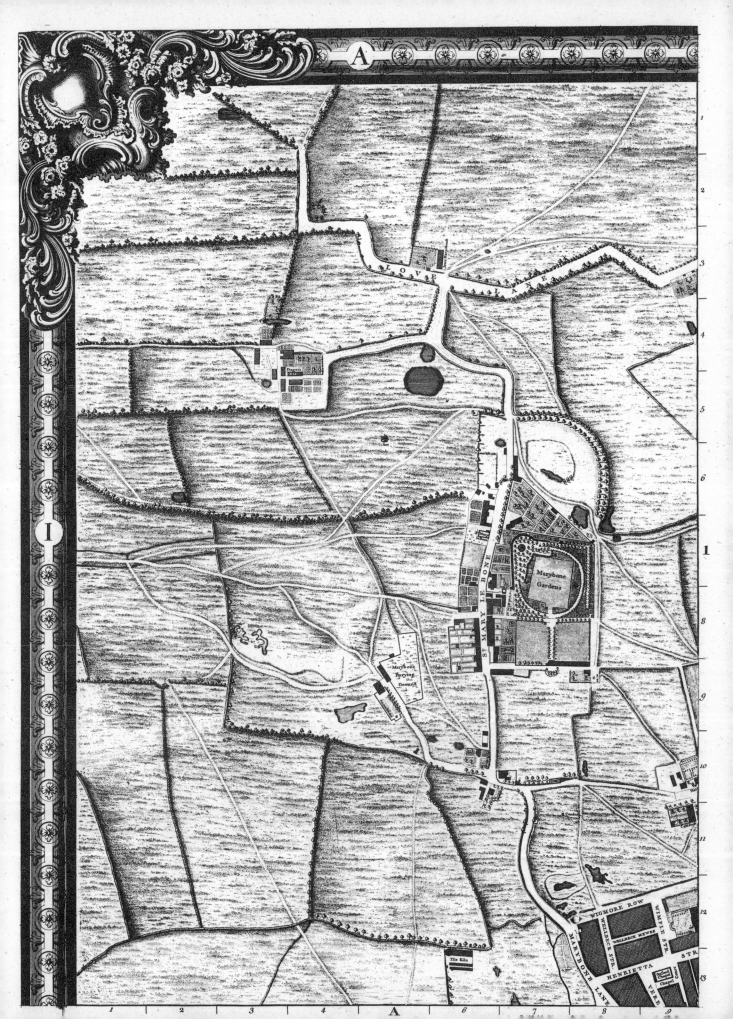

LOVE   LANE

Dagen's Vine

MARYBONE Gardens

ST MARY LE BONE

Marybone Burying Ground

Tile Kiln

WIGMORE ROW

WIMPOLE STR.

WELBECK MEWS

MARYBONE LANE

WELBECK STR.

HENRIETTA STR.

VERE

Oxford Chapel

I

TYBURN TO HYDE PARK CORNER

GROSVENOR SQUARE, begun in 1695 and by 1746 an aristocratic place of residence, is conspicuous in this west Section of our map. The famous Earl of Chesterfield was living in the square while his princely Chesterfield House was being completed. Dr. Johnson, having addressed to him the plan for his dictionary in the hope of his patronage, called on the Earl in 1749, only to be left in an " outward room," and later shown the door.

Half of Berkeley Square appears in this Section : the ground was laid out, but building was slow, and perhaps fitful. Robert Adam was to design it finally in 1765.

Meanwhile, Park Lane was still Tyburn Lane, and Oxford Street Tyburn Road. The Park was enclosed by an eight-feet wall. There is a turnpike at Hyde Park Corner, and a Park Lodge at the gate, with a milestone from which distances west from London were measured. This Lodge was to become Apsley House in 1785. St. George's Hospital had been founded near the turnpike in 1733, in converted Lanesborough House.

Knight's Bridge is spelled in its original form : there had been a bridge over the West Bourn from the earliest times, and the district, lying low, was subject to inundation when the stream became swollen from heavy rain. This happened in February 1737, when the flood carried away a portion of the Park wall. The West Bourn was supplying water to the Serpentine : not until 1834 was it diverted to a sewer.

George II had been king for twenty years in 1747. He had busied himself with the improvement of Kensington Gardens, then the private park of Kensington Palace. Queen Caroline had been interested in Hyde Park, and the Serpentine was formed at her direction. The King seconded her efforts by the construction of a new royal road to Kensington Palace, south of the road called " The King's Old Road." The latter became a favourite resort for carriages and saddle-horses, and later developed into the prepared horse-ride known as Rotten Row—rotten because of the material of which it was composed, to make it springy.

The circular reservoir of Chelsea Water Works will be noticed. It was 200 feet in diameter and was made in 1725 to supply the town and palace of Kensington, also the Mount Street area. There is a fountain in its place now. The avenues of trees are walnuts : planted when the reservoir was made, they were old and decayed by 1811 when they were cut down. Stocks for soldiers' muskets were made from the wood.

Almost opposite the reservoir, with its entrance in Upper Grosvenor Street, is Grosvenor House, mansion of the Duke of Westminster, bought later by George III's brother, the Duke of Gloucester.

At the top of Tyburn Lane, in Tyburn Road, is a turnpike much pictured in old prints. To the left again, inside the Park, is the place " where soldiers are shot." In the centre of the road crossing is Tyburn Gallows, or " Deadly Never Green." The name Tyburn was derived from The Aye Bourn, a small stream which rose near Hampstead and ran down east of this Section to the Thames near Westminster.

Tyburn Gallows was a place of execution from 1400 until 1738. There may have been a great tree here in early times, for the gallows was known as Tyburn Tree. When our map was made, and long before, it was a triangle of three tall perpendiculars, joined at the top. It appears to have been a permanent erection. Its site, a few feet to the south-west of the refuge at the south end of Edgware Road, is marked by a small metal triangle set in the road. The cart that conveyed the condemned from Newgate halted under the crossbars of the gallows, and drew away when he had been tied by the neck to one of them.

Perkin Warbeck (1499), Jack Sheppard (1724), Jonathan Wild (1725), and " Sixteen String Jack " (John Rann, 1774) were among the more notorious victims. Two hundred thousand saw Sheppard hanged ; many more watched Wild executed, " no more to be compared than a regiment to an army," according to Defoe.

Deserting soldiers were shot near Tyburn as unsparingly as civilians were hanged. In 1747 one Sergeant Smith was shot, then hanged on a gibbet : he had deserted, entered the French service, and afterwards that of the Pretender.

Duels, with pistols or swords, were common in the Park at this time. They often resulted in the death of one duellist or the other ; but in one combat the adversaries were said to have fired at one another over a distance of nearly a quarter of a mile ! They then " made it up."

Street names in the Grosvenor Square and Mayfair areas, have some points of interest. North Audley Street recalls Hugh Audley, a barrister of the Inner Temple who was also moneylender and miser. He amassed a fortune largely at the expense of improvident gallants ; also he foresaw the value of land in this area. He left nearly half a million.

Much of his property went to Thomas Davies, a bookseller in St. Paul's Churchyard, who was Lord Mayor in 1677 : Davies Street (misspelled " David " in our map) is named after him—or else, for the authorities differ, after the Miss Davies, heiress of Ebury Manor, who married Sir Thomas Grosvenor.

From the reign of Edward I a great fair was held every year in May or June, on ground occupied on our map by Chesterfield House, its gardens, Curzon Street, and the area south of it. Edward granted the privilege and profits of the fair, lasting a week, to the hospital of St. James the Less which occupied the site of St. James's Palace.

Pepys speaks of it as St. James's Fair. Later it was May Fair, and was notorious for " every enticement to low pleasure." Suppressed from time to time, it was as often revived, and persisted until 1809. At the time of our map Edward Shepherd, builder and owner of Shepherd's Market, had just died. In 1708 he paid one guinea ground rent, " of the Faire, market, and one house " : that guinea would scarcely pay for a square inch of land in Mayfair to-day.

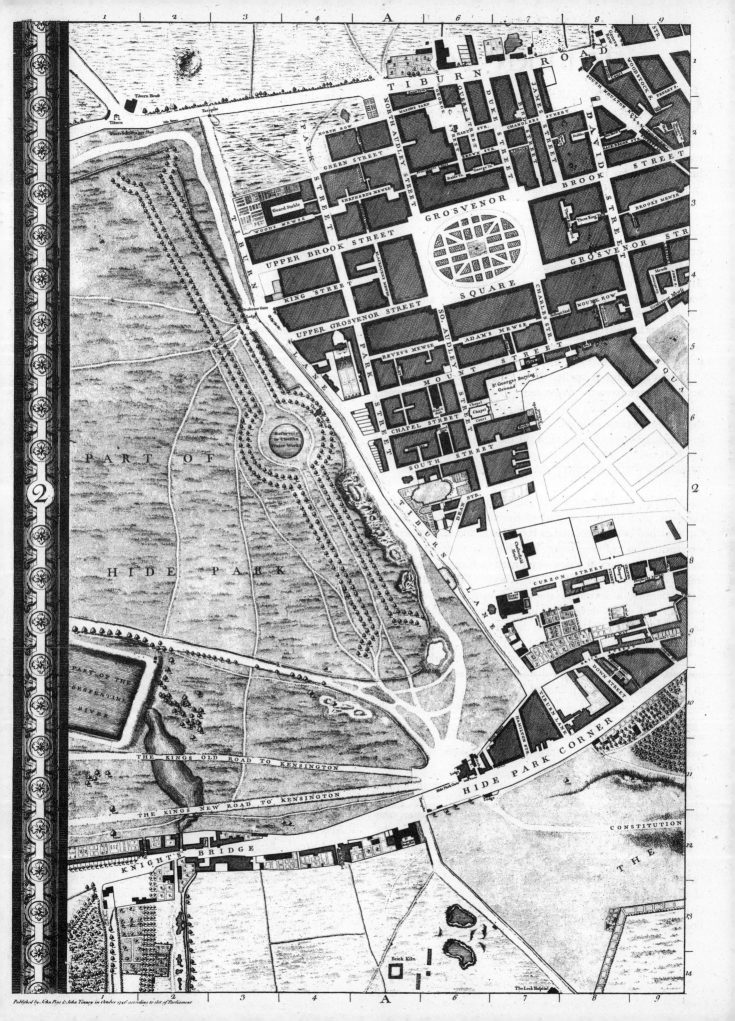

GIANT'S LANTHORN OF RANELAGH

IT is not easy to recognise, in this Section A 3, the portions of modern Belgravia and Chelsea which it represents. Thus, Eaton Square covers a considerable stretch of The King's Road, and Sloane Square has come in, at the bend in the road, level with the large figure 3 in the border on the left.

Sloane Street, running north-west from the Square, seems to have taken the place of a snaky, tree-lined footpath. Cadogan Place and Square, Lennox Gardens, Hans Place, and about half of Belgrave Square, not built until 1825, all arose in the fields of the upper half of this map during the early years of the nineteenth century.

Chelsea Road of our map can be traced as Buckingham Palace Road; Strumbelo is Pimlico Road; and Jews Row, continued past "Chelsea College," is Royal Hospital Road. The little Chelsea Bridge on our map is now Ebury Bridge, spanning Grosvenor Canal. Chelsea Water Works has become a pumping station of the Metropolitan Water Board.

That strange word "Strumbelo," appearing on our map as if it were a street name, implied buildings in that piece of what is now Pimlico Road. There was a tea garden there which had a fine fountain, and the name was probably taken from Stromboli, volcano of the Lipari Islands, Italy, which is continuously in a mild form of activity and is often called the Lighthouse of the Mediterranean.

Chelsea College is the old name of Chelsea Hospital for old and disabled soldiers: it had been a religious institution prior to 1682, when Charles II laid the foundation for Sir Christopher Wren's building.

The King's Road was still reserved for the private use of the Monarch and his Court on their passage to Kew and Hampton Court. Pass tickets of copper, with "The King's Private Roads, 1731" on one side and a crown and G.R. on the other, were granted to the favoured few. This King's Road was given up to the public in 1831.

Ranelagh Gardens strikes a dominant chord in social history. Diaries and letters of the period have many illuminating references to the place, for it was a gay and a fashionable resort for half a century. It was primarily a rendezvous of "the quality," the women in crinolines and bustles, the men in knee breeches, fine skirted coats, flowered waistcoats, and powdered wigs; but there was nothing to bar humbler folk, and they could mingle with lords and ladies in the pleasant gardens, or in the promenade of the Rotunda.

This, 150 feet in diameter, was the principal attraction. From without when lighted the Rotunda suggested to one contemporary writer, "a giant's lanthorn: the interior a vast amphitheatre gaily painted and gilded, forty-eight boxes in a double row, a magnificent orchestra in the centre." This was later moved to one side. The lighting was by chandeliers of candles in crystal glasses.

Boswell says Dr. Johnson declared "the *coup d'oeil* was the finest thing he had ever seen; and gave an expansion and gay sensation to his mind such as he never experienced anywhere else."

There was promenading in the arena—"talking scandal and quizzing one another"—and eating, drinking, and music in the boxes: "music of all kinds echoed, though not intelligently, from every one of those elegant retreats, where Pleasure seemed to beckon her wanton followers."

How Ranelagh impressed one seems to have depended on one's mood. This contemporary writer I quote was "familiar with the whole in five minutes; in the next five minutes indifference took place; in five more my eyes grew dazzled, my head became giddy."

Horace Walpole, on the other hand, went every night. "Ranelagh has totally beat Vauxhall," he says. "Nobody goes anywhere else—everybody goes there. My Lord Chesterfield is so fond of it that he says he has ordered all his letters to be directed thither . . . for the floor is all of beaten princes, that you can't set your foot without treading on a Prince of Wales or Duke of Cumberland." And such was the congestion on the road from Town that Walpole, going there one night, "in a string of coaches, we had a stop of 36 minutes."

Ranlagh disappeared in 1805, and no traces of the famous Rotunda, plainly seen on our map, now remain. The site was opposite the Barracks of the Brigade of Guards, and the Chelsea Bridge Road of to-day runs through the fringe of the old gardens.

The little Chelsea Bridge on our map leads into a road described "The Neat (i.e. Cow) Houses." Pasturage seems to have given place to market gardening, for two hundred years ago there were gardens here supplying London and Westminster markets "with Asparagus, Artichoaks, Cauliflowers, Musmelons, and the like useful things that the earth produceth "—to quote Strype, writing in 1720. Earlier, in Pepys's day, the Neat Houses were a place of resort which the diarist visited in 1667 and 1668. On the first occasion, "in a box in a tree, we sat and sang and eat."

Soil excavated from St. Katharine's Dock was dumped here in 1830 and the area was raised to the level of Chelsea Road (Buckingham Palace Road). Trains of the Southern Railway run in and out of Victoria Station where those market gardens lay.

The Rotunda, Ranelagh Gardens, in 1750

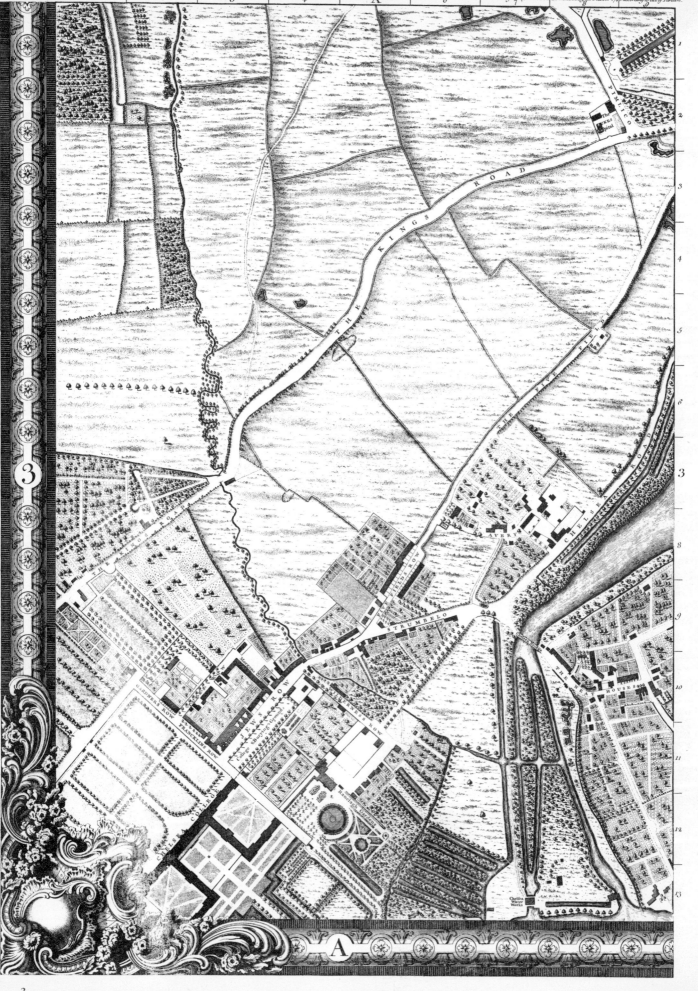

Publish'd by John Pine & John Tinney in October 1746 according to Act of Parliam.'

THE KINGS ROAD

PIMLICO

CHELSEA ROAD

THE FIVE FIELDS

AVERY

STRUMBELO

FIELDS ROW

JEWS ROW

FRANCKLIN ROW

CARDINALS ROW

CHELSEA COLLEGE

THE NECK HOUSES

Chelsea Water Works

A

NORTH OF OXFORD STREET

OXFORD CIRCUS had not been thought of when our map was drawn. It was to come seventy years later, with John Nash's Regent Street. Here George III's royal route from Carlton House, Pall Mall, to Regent's Park, replaced Balsover Street and Ogle Street to Mortimer Street, where Langham Place begins. Then comes Portland Place which, on our map, would run out of this Section on the left above the figure 1 in the margin.

At this point is the east end of Marylebone Road. Portland Street, now Great Portland Street, comes up parallel with Portland Place, and meets the junction of Marylebone Road, Albany Street, and Euston Road. At this cross-roads on our map stands Farthing Pie House, a noted place of entertainment, now the Green Man public-house; also Great Portland Street underground station.

Euston Road crosses Tottenham Court Road and can be traced in a faintly-marked footpath: Euston station is half-way between " Road to Highgate " and the eastern limit of this Section.

Tottenham Court Road is an old market road from St. Giles to Hampstead, Kentish Town, and Highgate. There was a manor of Tothill, Totenhall, or Totenham Court which in very early days belonged to the Dean and Chapter of St. Paul's. The Manor House stood at the cross-roads where there is now the Adam and Eve public-house. At the time of our map the Adam and Eve was a noted tea gardens. Outside it Hogarth laid the scene of " The March of the Guards to Finchley." There is a turnpike at the cross-roads, also a pound. Pound in this sense is the Anglo-Saxon *pund*, meaning enclosure : cattle distrained for rent, or caught straying and doing damage, came into custody of the law when put into a pound.

Broughton, the prize-fighter, who drew up the first rules of boxing, had an amphitheatre in the tea gardens about the time of our map, which he called the Tottenham Court Nursery. He announced of a lecture here that it would be illustrated by " the nature of blows, stops, cross-buttocks, etc., the whole leading to the most successful method of beating a man deaf, dumb, lame, and blind." The lecturers were " Thomas Smallwood, Gymnast of St. Giles's, and Thomas Dimmock, Athleta of Southwark." Broughton also had an amphitheatre in Hanway Yard, near Oxford Street.

Half-way along Tottenham Court Road on the left-hand side is a little group of buildings called Paradise Row. Near to them George Whitefield was to build his second tabernacle in 1756. At the time our map was made he was in the United States, but he was soon to return and become chaplain to the Countess of Huntingdom.

Lower down the thoroughfare is Windmill Street, where Middlesex Hospital had just been opened in a small house. Another site was soon found in the Marylebone Fields at the end of Berners Street, where the great hospital stands to-day.

The " Mary Bone Place " on our map is now Wells Street. Rathbone Place leads to Merchants Water Works, all trace of which has disappeared. Joseph Nollekens, the sculptor, was taken as a small boy, about the date of our map, to walk " by the side of a long pond near a windmill." A halfpenny was paid to the miller for the privilege of walking in his grounds.

Cavendish Square was still not completed two hundred years ago, its north side being reserved for the stately mansion of the princely-minded Duke of Chandos. He had been Paymaster of the Forces in Queen Anne's reign and had amassed an immense fortune. He had already built Canons, a palatial mansion near Edgware, Middlesex, at a cost of £250,000. Few sovereign princes lived in such style, with music at every meal, and a flourish of trumpets to herald the next course. He rebuilt Little Stanmore church as his chapel, and Handel was his choirmaster.

Only the wings of the London mansion he projected in Cavendish Square were built, joined by a handsome wall and gates. He lost his fortune by speculation, notably in the South Sea Bubble, and the splendour of Canons was much diminished before he died in 1744. Chandos Street, in the north-east corner of the Square, preserves a memory of the Duke.

Soho Square, part of which is in this Section, dates back to 1681. Strype refers to it as " a stately quadrate designated King's Square, but vulgarly Soho Square." It was aristocratic two hundred years ago, and consisted of fine houses. The name So-ho, an old cry of huntsmen used when a hare was found, belonged to the district.

The High Street, in the right-hand bottom corner of this Section, is that of St. Giles-in-the-Fields, so named to distinguish it from St. Giles, Cripplegate. Hog Lane, beside it, is the northern end of Charing Cross Road. There was a parish boundary stone here : when the charity boys of St. Giles's parish walked the boundaries, " those who have deserved flogging are whipp'd at this stone, in order that as they grow up they may remember the place, and be competent to give evidence should any dispute arise with the adjoining parishes."

Part of Old Tottenham Court

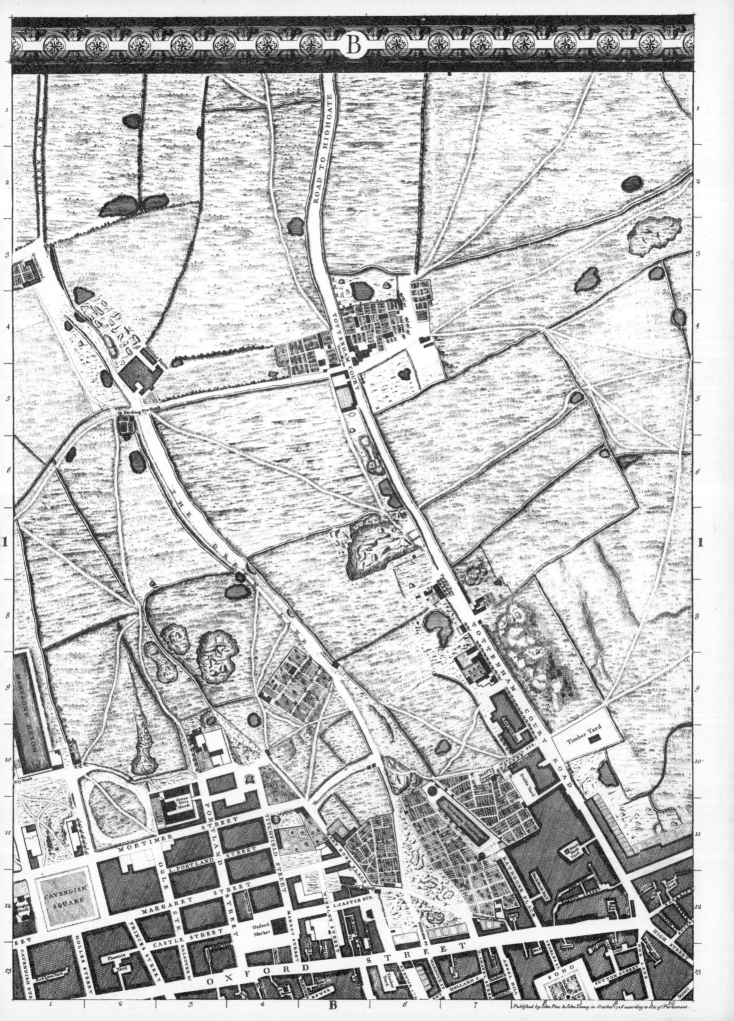

ROAD TO HIGHGATE

TOTTENHAM COURT

THE DREN

TOTTENHAM COURT ROAD

Farthing Pye Houfe

Timber Yard

MARY-BONE PARISH

Whg Houfe

Green Acre Mead

Stable Yard

MidI's
Court

Ratbone
Yard

MORTIMER

PORTLAND STREET

OGLE STREET

L. PORTLAND STREET

STREET

TITCHFIELD STREET

RATHBONE PLACE

RATHBONE PLACE

CAVENDISH SQUARE

MARGARET STREET

MARKET STREET

L. CASTLE STR.

SOHO

CAVENDISH SQ.

HOLLES STREET

PRINCES STREET

CASTLE STREET

BALSOVER ST.

Phoenix Yard

Oxford Market

Timber Yard

HOLLAND

HIGH STREET

OXFORD STREET

Published by John Pine & John Tinney in October 1746 according to Act of Parliament.

MASKED SUPPERS IN HANOVER SQUARE

THIS looks more like modern London than some other sections of our map. To bring it up to date one need only place Piccadilly Circus at the junction of Piccadilly, the Haymarket, and Coventry Street; bring Regent Street up from Pall Mall, through Alban's Street and St. James's Market to Piccadilly; swing it round (Nash's Quadrant) to Little Swallow Street, and continue it along Great Swallow Street to Oxford Circus—just outside the border of this Section.

Also, Shaftesbury Avenue, made in 1886, must be put in, swinging northwards in a curve from Piccadilly Circus to Richmond Street and King Street at the side of St. Anne's Church, Soho.

In the north-west corner of the Section is Hanover Square, built about 1718, fashionable at the time of our map. Lady Mary Wortley Montague is credited with an account of a private society which met at Lord Hillsborough's in Hanover Square about 1730, "where each gentleman came masked, and brought with him one lady—either his mistress, or any other man's wife, or perhaps a woman of the town—who was also masked. They were on oath not to divulge names, and continued masked the whole time." The purpose of this genteel society seems to have been supper and flirtation.

Leicester Fields, with Leicester House and its garden on the north side, has changed much to become Leicester Square. In 1718 when the Prince of Wales, the future George II, had quarrelled with his father and had been told to quit

Hanover Square in 1750

St. James's Palace, he bought Leicester House and lived in it: here his son, the Duke of Cumberland, hero of Culloden, was born. In the next reign there was a breach between George II and his son, Frederick Prince of Wales, whereupon the Prince made Leicester House his home as his father had done in similar circumstances before him.

Hogarth was living on the east side of Leicester Fields during 1733–1756. One of his sitters on leaving offered the painter's servant a small gratuity. "The man very politely refused it," he relates, "telling me it would be as much as the loss of his place if his master knew it. This was so uncommon and so liberal in a man of Hogarth's profession at that time of day, that it much struck me, as nothing of the kind had happened to me before."

It will be seen that Burlington House, built for Richard Boyle, second Earl of Cork and first Earl of Burlington, had a very spacious garden behind it in 1746. The owner then was the great grandson of the first Earl, and he gave the mansion a new front, a porch, colonnade, and gateway, all much admired when they were new. The colonnade was sacrificed when new wings round a spacious quadrangle were built on the Piccadilly front in 1866. On the site of the garden at the back was erected about the same time the University of London, now the Civil Service Commission and the British Academy.

The parks were more picturesque than the map suggests. A contemporary drawing of Rosamond's Pond surroundings shows that they were charming. The long stretch of water that is now the lake in St. James's Park, certainly was as formal in shape as a canal, which is what it was called. But its banks must have been pleasant, and it was well stocked with a variety of waterfowl.

The tree-shaded Mall was the fashionable promenade of Court and society folk—handsomely dressed, painted and powdered. Constitutional Hill, not yet a roadway, was used for walking exercise, notably by Queen Caroline; but she, of course, died ten years before our map was made.

George II, hero of Dettingen, loved to see his troops paraded. There are records of royal reviews of dragoon regiments in 1747, held in the Green Park near Queen Caroline's library, which was on the site of Stafford House at the south-west corner of St. James's Palace. One regiment "was complete, excepting about 24 men who are either dead or sick, and their horses were led with boots hanging to their saddles . . . the toes of the boots of the sick men were pointed to the horses' heads, and those of the dead men to their tails."

Buckingham House, built in 1705 for John Sheffield, Duke of Buckingham and Normandy, politician and poet, stood till 1825, and was not a royal residence until 1762, when George III bought it from the Duke's son. The present Palace was a reconstruction on the same site from John Nash's designs, but many alterations and additions have been made since.

Published by John Pine & John Tinney in October 1746 according to Act of Parliament.

FROM PAUPERISM TO CRIME

VICTORIA STREET, opened in 1851, begins at the east end of Tothill Street at the top of this Section. It curves down past the top corner of Artillery Ground, and across to Victoria Station, which lies just above the Chelsea Water Works on the left-hand of the Section.

From Victoria Station, Vauxhall Bridge Road swings in a south-easterly direction across the Section, leaving it at the space between fields on the right-hand side.

Tothill Street, Broadway, and James Street survive to-day, the latter as Buckingham Gate; so do most of the streets in the right-hand top corner—Pye, Orchard, and Peter Streets, and "Road to the Horse Ferry." The site of the ferry, now Lambeth Bridge, is in the adjacent Section C 3.

Rochester Row in Tothill Fields remains, and the series of almshouses it comprised—with a row of trees before them as regular as a file of soldiers on parade, is now United Westminster Almshouses, rebuilt in 1881.

Artillery Ground was a large enclosure "made use of by those who delight in military exercises." At the time of our map there were butts for musketry practice. Opposite the south-west corner of the enclosure is the Grey Coat Hospital, a school founded in 1698 which still flourishes, despite Hitler's fire bombs in 1941. They burned out its board room, the school hall of the Tudor wing, and brought down the old roof with its fine turret. This is now a distinguished secondary school for girls, though it retains its old name of hospital.

In the James Street of our map is Lady Dacre's Almshouses, founded 1594, and round the corner, beside Bridewell, is Green Coat School, dating from 1633. Neither building exists to-day, but the charities survive, the aged people being in the care of the Lord Mayor and Aldermen of the City of London, the children's interests being represented by Emanuel School, Wandsworth.

Bridewell also dates from 1633: it is not to be confused with Bridewell in the City. Probably this Bridewell and the Green Coat School, originally called St. Margaret's Hospital, were joint parish institutions, the one for the employment of indolent paupers, the other for fatherless children.

It was a short step from pauperism and vagrancy to crime, and like the great house Bridewell in Bride Lane, presented by Edward VI to the City of London as a workhouse for the poor, this Bridewell became a house of correction, and finally a criminal prison as well.

Tothill Fields, covering the whole of this Section, was a manor in Westminster in early times: the word is toot-hill, a natural, or artificial, hill or mound used for a look-out place. Two hundred years ago there were fields right down to the river, and in the right-hand bottom corner in what is now Grosvenor Road, are Neat, or Cow Houses. The closely-populated districts of Belgrave Road, St. George's Road, and Lupus Street now cover these fields, constituting a large part of once-fashionable Pimlico.

A small piece of the fields remains to-day in the cricket and football grounds of Westminster School in Vincent Square, which in our map falls opposite the Almshouses of Rochester Row. There was a bear garden on the site until 1793.

BEATING HEMP IN BRIDEWELL

From Hogarth's original engraving; this illustration refers to the City Bridewell and not the Bridewell mentioned above

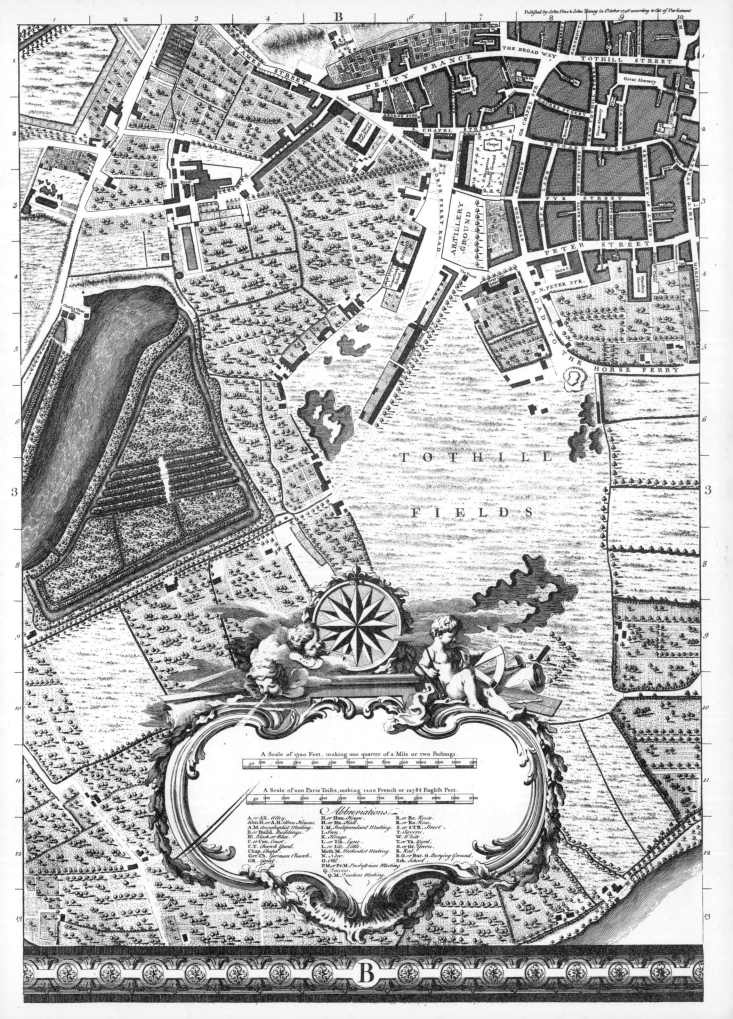

Publish'd by John Pine & John Tinney in October 1746 according to Act of Parliament

B

1 2 3 4 B 5 6 7 8 9 10

JAMES STREET

PETTY FRANCE

THE BROAD WAY

TOTHILL STREET

Great Almnery

L. CHAPEL STREET

GR. CHAPEL STR.

DAVIS'S STREET

Chapel

ORCHARD STREET

NEW WAY

ARTILLERY GROUND

HORSE FERRY ROAD

STRETTON GROUNDS

DUCK LANE

PYE STREET

PETER STREET

N. PETER STR.

MARIAN

ROAD TO THE HORSE FERRY

TOTHILL

FIELDS

Abbreviations.

A. or All. Alley.
Alm.H. or A.H. Alms Houses.
A.M. Anabaptist Meeting.
B. or Build. Buildings.
C. or Cou. Court.
C.Y. Church Yard.
Chap. Chapel.
Ger.Ch. German Church.
GR. Great.

H. or Hou. House.
H. or Ha. Hall.
I.M. Independant Meeting.
Inn.
K. Kings.
L. or Lh. Lane.
L. or Lit. Little.
Meth.M. Methodist Meeting.
N. or Nr.
O. Old.
P.M. or Pr.M. Presbyterian Meeting.
Q. Queens.
Q.M. Quakers Meeting.

R. or Re. Rents.
R. or Ro. Row.
S. or STR. Street.
T. Tavern.
W. White.
Y. or Ya. Yard.
G. or Gr. Green.
R. Red.
B.G. or Bur. G. Burying Ground.
Sch. School.

A Scale of 1320 Feet, making one quarter of a Mile or two Furlongs.

A Scale of 200 Paris Toises, making 1200 French or 1278½ English Feet.

B

BLOOMSBURY AND ITS SQUARES

LAMBS CONDUIT FIELDS—the words fall pleasantly on the ear—seem to dominate this Section. In their place to-day we have Russell Square, a portion of the Parcels Post office at Mount Pleasant, the Royal Free Hospital in Gray's Inn Road, a portion of St. Pancras Station, and a network of bustling, busy streets.

William Lambe, who in 1577 caused several springs to be connected so as to form a head of water, run thence in lead pipes to a conduit on Snow Hill, 2000 yards distant, was Master of the Clothworkers Company in 1569, and a benefactor in many directions.

These fields abounded in springs. Black Mary's Hole, or Well, was one. Black Mary is said to have been a woman of dark complexion, named Woolaston, who in 1680 lived in a hut by the well and sold the water, chiefly to soldiers camping in adjacent fields. Part of King's Cross Road runs along the road called Black Mary's Hole on our map.

The Foundling Hospital, just opened two hundred years ago, displaced Mr. Lambe's original conduit, which was moved to Red Lion Street, now a part of Lamb's Conduit Street. Captain Thomas Coram, master of a trading vessel, founded the Hospital, " for exposed and deserted children," after seventeen years of frustrated endeavour. Unwanted children were deposited in a basket at the gate after ringing a bell to give notice to the Hospital staff.

Coram's great friend was Hogarth, who greatly assisted him. He painted Coram's portrait and presented it with other pictures to the Hospital. These were shown to the public and became an attraction. Other artists then gave pictures, and out of this exhibition grew the first Royal Academy show in the Adelphi in 1760. Meantime, a visit to the Foundling became the fashionable morning occupation of society, and the grounds in front of the Hospital were a favourite promenade.

Another Foundling benefactor was Handel, whose " Messiah " when played in the Hospital chapel enriched the funds by £1000 a time. He bequeathed the score to the Foundling. The Hospital is now at Berkhamsted as the Thomas Coram Schools, and part of the site it occupies on our map became a children's playground in 1932, thanks to the first Lord Rothermere and other donors.

The High Holborn of our map is now continued westwards to the corner of Hart Street, where New Oxford Street begins. Above Hart Street is Montague House, built 1687. Bought by the Government in 1753, it was demolished to build the British Museum. Bedford House, originally built for Thomas Wriothesley, Earl of Southampton, remained until 1800. Its grounds extended to Russell Square : Bedford Street now runs through the site of house and grounds.

Gray's Inn Road now extends to the top of this Section, where it joins Pentonville and Euston roads in front of King's Cross Station. Gray's Inn is seen with its divisions bearing their original names—Coney Court, Holborn Court, Field Court, and Chapel Court. Raymond's Buildings and Verulam Buildings had not been built.

Lincoln's Inn consisted of Old Square, with its Hall and gateway, and New Square : New Hall and Library were added in 1843, Stone Buildings in 1845.

The theatre seen in Portugal Street (parallel with Portugal Row) is the third Lincoln's Inn Theatre, by this time a repository. John Rich had introduced pantomime here, he playing Harlequin. In 1727, Gay's *The Beggar's Opera* at its first performance here was so successful that it was said to make Rich Gay and Gay Rich.

Red Lion Square, named after a famous Holborn inn, had just been enclosed with iron railings, with a stone watch-house at each corner, and a plain obelisk in the centre, as our map shows. This was an effort to beautify the Square ; but the watch-houses resembled family vaults, and the obelisk was likened to " the sad monument of a disconsolate widow for the loss of her first husband."

GRAY'S INN
—from an old engraving

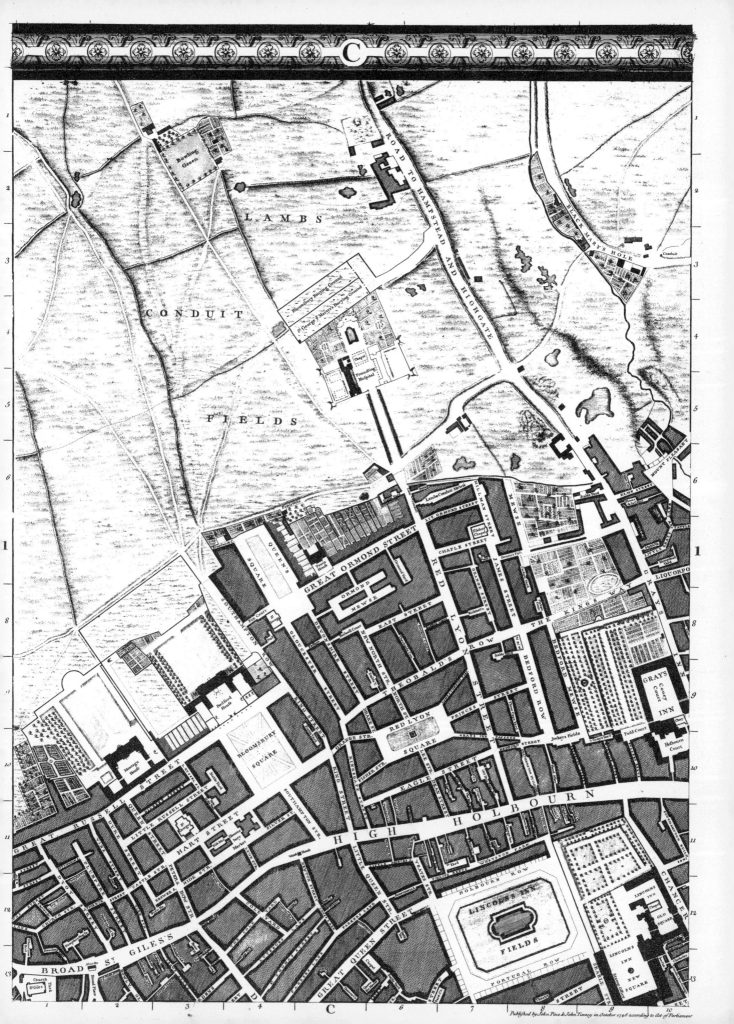

LAMBS

CONDUIT

FIELDS

Bowling Green

ROAD TO HAMPSTEAD AND HIGHGATE

BLACK MARYS HOLE

Conduit

Bloomsbury Burying Ground

St George & St Mary's Burying Ground

Chapel

Foundling Hospital

MOUNT PLEASANT

QUEENS SQUARE

GREAT ORMOND STREET

Lambs Conduit Newells

GREAT ORMOND STREET

GILMAN STREET

CHAPLE STREET

RED LYON ROW

JAMES STREET

THE KINGS WAY

BEDFORD MEWES

GRAYS INN

LIQUORPOND

ORMOND MEWSE

EAST STREET

BEDFORD ROW

GRAYS INN

Conny Court

SOUTHAMPTON

Bedford House

RED LYON SQUARE

Jockeys Fields

Field Court

Holbourn Court

BLOOMSBURY SQUARE

KING STREET

EAGLE STREET

HIGH HOLBOURN

Montague House

RUSSELL STREET

LITTLE RUSSELL STREET

HART STREET

SOUTHAMPTON STR.

HOLBOURN ROW

CHANCERY

LINCOLNS INN

LINCOLN'S INN FIELDS

GREAT QUEEN STREET

PORTUGAL ROW

LINCOLN'S INN NEW SQUARE

ST GILES'S

BROAD ST GILES'S

Church St Giles

Publish'd by John Pine & John Tinney in October 1746 according to Act of Parliament

SAVOY PALACE IN DECAY

MANY changes have come to this Section. We have to place Kingsway and Aldwych; the Victoria Embankment; Waterloo Bridge and Station; Waterloo Road; Charing Cross railway and footbridge, and Station; the County Hall; Trafalgar Square and the National Gallery; Northumberland Avenue; and Government offices in Parliament Street and Whitehall.

What remained two hundred years ago of the Savoy, a great house or palace in the thirteenth century, and a hospital of St. John the Baptist, 1505–1702, is contained on our map between Somerset Water Gate and Savoy Stairs, and the Embankment passes over a part of it. Strype in 1720 tells of a " very ruinous building," with a great hall, the walls three feet thick, the roof in many places open to the weather.

" This large Hall is now divided into several apartments," Strype continues. " A cooper hath part of it. . . . Other parts serve for keeping Prisoners as Deserters, men prest for military service, Dutch recruits, etc. . . . In this Savoy, how ruinous soever it is, are divers good houses. First the King's Printing Press . . . next a Prison; thirdly a Parish Church (Savoy Chapel), and churches for the French, for Dutch, for High Germans and Lutherans, and for the Protestant Dissenters. Here be also harbours for many refugees and poor people."

The Savoy continued to be a refuge for debtors and disorderly persons long after sanctuary was annulled, and the Chapel of the Hospital, now the Chapel Royal of the Savoy, was notorious until 1754 for clandestine marriages. Only this chapel remains, the rest of the Savoy buildings being demolished for the approaches to Waterloo Bridge.

This (i.e. the original) Waterloo Bridge was opened in 1817. It spans the river from slightly east of Somerset Water Gate to Cuper's Bridge. Waterloo Road runs through the centre of Cuper's Gardens, and the Station spreads itself between those gardens and the Vine Street of our map. The railway rides over the New Road, now called Westminster Bridge Road.

The National Gallery is on the site of the Royal Mews, where the King's hawks were kept from the fourteenth century as long as falconry was a royal pastime. About 1534 the premises were rebuilt for the stabling of the King's horses, but they retained the name of mews (i.e. cage for hawks when moulting).

Butcher Row, a good market for meat, also noted for its inns and for eating-houses used by Dr. Johnson, was pulled down in 1813, and Pickett Street was erected in its stead. This was removed in 1874 when the Law Courts were built.

Holywell Street, a picturesque, narrow lane of mercers' shops, later of second-hand book shops, was swept away when Aldwych was constructed. Kingsway begins where Stanhope Street and Drury Lane meet on our map, and cuts in a north-westerly direction through a cluster of small streets.

Charing Cross Hotel and Station occupy the place of Hungerford Market, between Villiers Street and Craven Street. Sir Edward Hungerford of Farleigh Castle, Somersetshire, built the market-place of our map in 1680 from his town house and grounds.

Northumberland House was bought by the Government in 1873, and demolished to make way for Northumberland Avenue. Grand Buildings and the Constitutional Club occupy part of the site. Built in 1605 by the first Earl of Northampton, this magnificent mansion became Suffolk House in 1615 on passing to the first Earl of that ilk, and Northumberland House in 1642, when it became the town house of the Percy family.

Near to the gardens of Northumberland House is Scotland Yard, with its Middle and Inner sections. The name is derived from ambassadors and kings of Scotland having lodged there. Stow refers to this residential area simply as " Scotland." Here for many years were the offices of the Police Commissioners. Great Scotland Yard, a street connecting Northumberland Avenue to Whitehall, recalls this area. Present headquarters of the Metropolitan Police, off Parliament Street, is New Scotland Yard.

In the left-hand top corner of the Section is Seven Dials, the 30-feet column in the centre. It had only six sun dials, so two of the streets radiating from it shared one of them. The column is now on Weybridge Green.

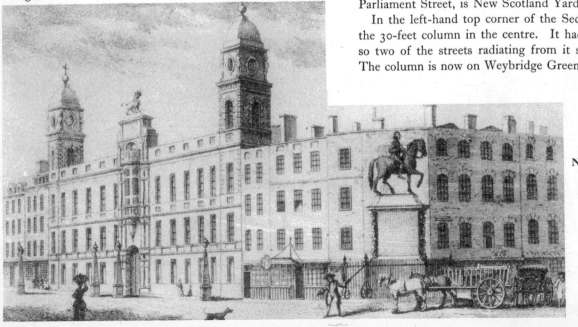

NORTHUMBERLAND HOUSE AND CHARING CROSS

—from an old engraving

LADY CAROLINE AT VAUXHALL GARDENS

ST. PETER'S ABBEY in the north-west corner of this Section is Westminster Abbey, much as it is to-day, for additions to the western towers were completed in 1739. The Houses of Parliament, however, were the low, rambling buildings destroyed by fire in 1834.

Two centuries ago the Commons were meeting in the adapted chapel of St. Stephen (at right angles to Westminster Hall). Its gothic roof was hidden by a false ceiling and its walls were covered by oak panels. The crypt of this chapel survived the fire, and is now used for christenings and marriages in the families of M.P.'s. The Lords sat in a part of the Court of Requests, which was beside St. Stephen's and had an entrance in Old Palace Yard.

To-day the Houses of Parliament extend to the river, and half-way along Abingdon Street. Victoria Tower Gardens, laid out in 1881, occupy the river bank as far as Market Street where Lambeth Bridge now spans the river.

Here was the only horse ferry allowed on the Thames at or near London. At the time of our map it was still functioning as such, for Westminster Bridge, nearly completed, was not opened until 1750. The tolls and right of passage belonged by patent to the Archbishop of Canterbury. The rates were, for a man and a horse, 2s.; horse and chaise, 1s.; coach and two horses, 1s. 6d.; coach and four horses, 2s.; coach and six horses, 2s. 6d.; cart loaded, 2s. 6d., unloaded, 2s. So when Westminster Bridge was opened to traffic the Archbishop was paid £3000 as compensation for the loss of these tolls.

Mill Bank ends on our map at Grosvenor House, residence of the Grosvenor family until 1809. It had a large courtyard in front and a fine garden behind, but was considered " not over healthful " by Strype because of the low-lying meadows south and west of it. A mill formerly occupied its site.

This section of Millbank is now incorporated in Grosvenor Road, which continues along the river bank past Vauxhall Bridge and on to Chelsea Embankment. Queen Alexandra's Military Hospital, the Tate Gallery, and the R.A.M.C. barracks occupy the once low-lying fields.

On the other side of the river the Albert Embankment, begun in 1865, extends from the top of the Section down three parts of its length, leading away from the river bank (near the point of the arrow in mid-stream) to join the street called Vaux Hall.

St. Thomas's Hospital now covers the area which is described on our map as Stangate. Behind it is Lambeth Marsh, now Upper Marsh, beside an area of fields divided by broad deep ditches, willow-bordered, and crossed by planks and narrow bridges. At the north end of Lower Marsh the Canterbury Music Hall was to appear later.

Of Lambeth Palace only the habitable portion and the Guard Chamber are comparatively new, having been re-built 1829–34. St. Mary's Church, beside the Palace, has been re-built, except the tower which dates from 1377. Church Street is now Lambeth Road, and leads to Bethlehem Hospital (Bedlam), moved to St. George's Fields in 1815, and now the Imperial War Museum. Lambeth Butts on our map is Broad Street and Princes Road; and Three Coney Walk is now Lambeth Walk, of dance-tune fame.

At Plate Glass House, Vaux Hall, plate-glass for mirrors and coach windows was made, 1670–1780, " so as to excel the Venetians, or any other nation, in blown plate-glass." Vauxhall " plates " were put into the Speaker's coach. Vauxhall crossing occupies the site of the factory.

Vauxhall Gardens were enjoying their successful middle period at the time of our map, and for a concert in 1749 there was an audience of 12,000. " So great a resort occasioned such a stoppage at London Bridge," the *Gentleman's Magazine* says of that night, " that no carriage could pass for three hours."

Horace Walpole tells of Lady Caroline Petersham's party in a booth at Vauxhall on a night in June 1750. The guests minced seven chickens, " which Lady Caroline stewed over a lamp with three pats of butter and a flagon of water, stirring and rattling and laughing, and we expecting the dish to fly about our ears. She had brought Betty the fruit-girl, with hampers of strawberries and cherries from Rogers's, and made her wait upon us . . . the whole air of our party was sufficient, as you will easily imagine, to take up the whole attention of the Garden."

Fountains played and nightingales sang in the shady walks, in competition with the " best band of musick in England." There were 1000 lamps, " so disposed that they all take fire together, almost as quick as lightning, and dart such a sudden blaze as is perfectly surprising." And surprising it must have been in 1751 when this description was written.

WESTMINSTER BRIDGE
AND ABBEY

—from the original pen and wash drawing by Canaletto, 1747

Published by John Pine & John Tinney in October 1746 according to Act of Parliament

C

THE BROAD
Church Yard
St Margaret

ST PETER'S ABBY

DEANS
YARD

Colt Cleg.
Gar? den

COLLEGE STREET

COWLEY STREET

WOOD STREET

VINE STREET

St John Evan.
Church Yard

MARKET STREET

St John's
Burying
Ground

MILL BANK

OLD PALACE YARD
ABINGDON STR.

Barracks
Yard

Parliament Stairs

The Horse Ferry

Stangate Stairs

Lambeth Palace

Chapel
St Mary
Lambeth Church Yard

Lambeth Stairs

LAMBETH CHURCH

The Horse Ferry

PARADISE ROW

Kings Head Yard

White Hart Stairs

The Pot House

LAMBETH

Gun house Stairs

Pot House

NEW ST.

Vaux Hall Stairs

VAUX HALL

PLATE GLASS
HOUSE

Marble Hall

Vaux Hall Spring Garden

LAMBETH MARSH

THREE

KENNINGTON

C

BARBARIC SPORT AND FIGHTING WOMEN

OF changes in this Section since 1746, most important are the construction of (a) Farringdon Road down Coppice Row, on the right of Saffron Hill, to Holborn and (as Farringdon Street) down Fleet Market; of (b) Holborn Viaduct, which bridges Farringdon Street and joins Holborn Hill to Newgate Street; of (c) Old Street westwards across Goswell Road, where it becomes Clerkenwell Road.

Smithfield (the "West" in our map is to distinguish it from East Smithfield elsewhere) is a model meat market to-day, but it was a huge market for live cattle and sheep two hundred years ago, and included horrible slaughter-houses.

South-east of Smithfield is St. Bartholomew's Hospital (11–7), still in that place. It was the earliest hospital for the sick, founded in 1123, and had a medical school before 1662.

Lower down, off Newgate Street, is Christ's Hospital (12–7/8), where the General Post Office now stands. This was first a hospital for poor fatherless children, founded by Edward VI in 1553; it became known as the Blue Coat School, and has developed into one of the great English schools. At Horsham, Sussex, whither it moved in 1902, the boys still wear the blue gown, of the same age as the foundation of the Hospital, yellow stockings, and a clergyman's band round the neck.

To the left of Christ's Hospital, bestriding Newgate Street, is New Gate itself, a City gate that was also, from the twelfth century, a prison. It remained until 1767, a dreadful place, badly ventilated, ill supplied with water, and always overcrowded. The Sessions House, forerunner of the Central Criminal Court (" the Old Bailey ") of to-day, adjoined the gate. Sixty persons died of New Gate gaol distemper in the spring of 1750, and they included two Judges, the Lord Mayor, and several of the Jury engaged in the Sessions House.

Above Smithfield Bars (9–6), in the broad part of St. John Street, is Hicks's Hall (8–6), the Sessions House of the County of Middlesex. It was named after Sir Baptist Hicks, a Cheapside Mercer, who built it in 1612. It is interesting because the distance on the milestones of the Great North Road were originally measured from it.

By our standards, much of this London, even less than two hundred years ago, was barbaric. In 1787 a writer of the period saw a man pilloried and pelted on Clerkenwell Green (6/7–4/5), and in Red Lyon Street, leading into the Green, he saw another flogged at the cart's tail.

Near to the Green was Hockley in the Hole (6/7–2/3), most of which disappeared in the making of Farringdon Road. Here was a bear garden for the cruel sport of baiting bears and bulls with dogs, and for prize fights in which the contestants occasionally were women. In 1772 Elizabeth Wilkinson and Hannah Fyfield, having "had words," fought in public for a stake of three guineas. To prevent scratching the women had to hold half a crown in each hand, and the first that dropped the money was to lose the battle.

Prominent at the top of this Section is the New River Head, reservoir of the pioneer New River Water Company that is now merged in the Metropolitan Water Board. The so-called river is an artificial course beginning at Chadwell Springs, between Hertford and Ware. It runs for several miles parallel to the river Lea. Sir Hugh Myddleton projected and completed it, 1608–13.

Defoe, writing in 1726, says it was supplying the greater part of the City with water then, " only . . . they have been obliged to dig a new head or basin at Islington on a higher ground . . . and this higher basin they fill from the lower, by a great engine formerly with six sails, now by many horses constantly working."

Beside the New River Head is New Tunbridge Wells, where to-day is the theatre called Sadler's Wells. Below its stage the spring can still be seen. Sadler was a surveyor of the highways when he discovered it in 1683. He opened in connection with it a music room he called " Sadler's Wells Music House." The water of the well was said to resemble that of Tunbridge Wells. At the time of our map drinking the waters cost threepence, and in the house of entertainment nearby during the summer season, " people are amused with balance-masters walking on the wire, rope-dancing, tumbling, and pantomime." The historic days of Grimaldi, the clown, of T. P. Cooke in *Black-Eyed Susan*, and of the great actor Phelps, were yet to come here.

Sadler's Wells in 1756

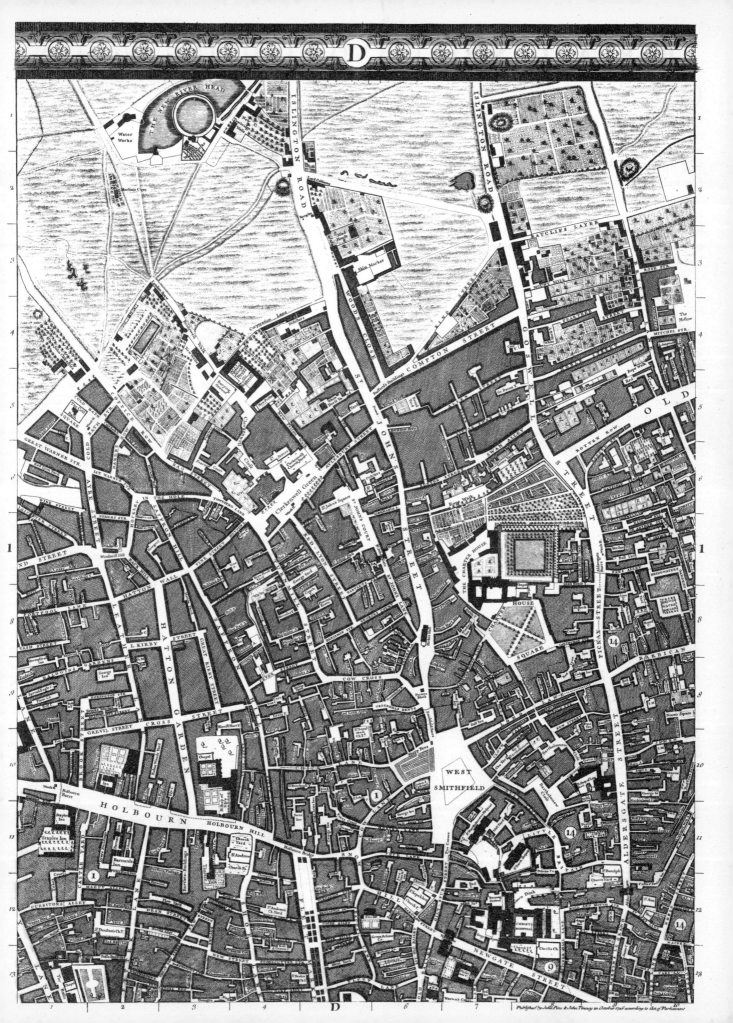

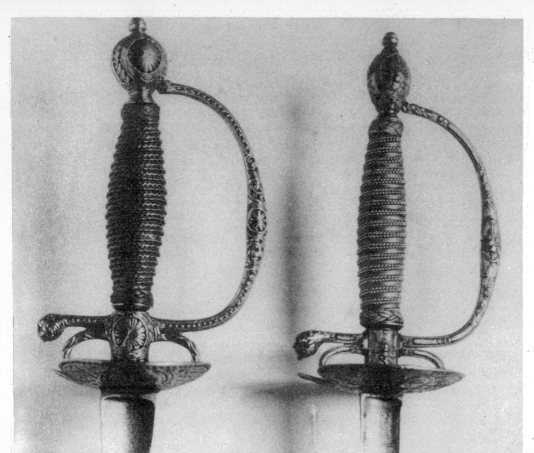

By courtesy of M. R. Holmes, F.S.A.

Swords and Pistols

A gentleman of our period was incompletely dressed without a sword: this is true to-day of a gentleman in Court dress.

Small-sword hilts and scabbards were as elegant as the clothes with which they were worn. The small-sword is similar to the rapier used in modern fencing. The blade is triangular in section, the sides are concave for lightness with rigidity, and the damage is done with the point. But though the small-sword might be worn for ornament it was capable of inflicting mortal hurt.

A notable duel was fought with small-swords in Hyde Park on November 15, 1712, which resulted in the death of both combatants. Lord Mohun, a notorious duellist, was killed on the spot, and his adversary, the Duke of Hamilton, died as he was being carried to his coach. The duel forms an incident in Thackeray's "Esmond."

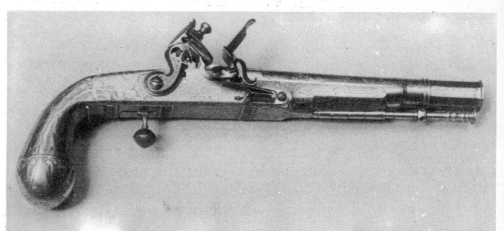

It behoved every man of spirit to be skilled in swordmanship. Swords were often drawn indoors, in the hot exchanges of a quarrel over the gaming tables, or to uphold the honour of a lady's name, and, in the street, in defence against sudden attack. The old men of the Watch, the police of the time, were seldom competent to protect the citizen against desperate ruffians.

Pistols were carried in the belt on a journey, and frequently were needed.

By courtesy of the Victoria and Albert Museum.

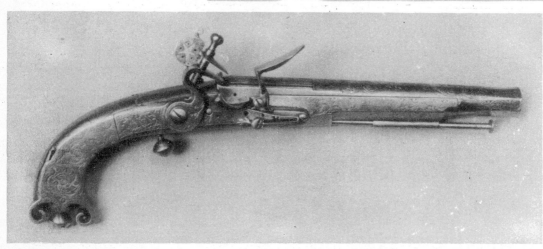

When journeying to Sadler's Wells, for instance, and to many another resort in what was then the country, over lonely, unlighted roads, travellers were liable to be set upon by highwaymen and robbed of purses and trinkets.

Duelling with pistols was common, but for the formal affair a case of duelling pistols were carried to the scene — finer weapons than the protective pistol stuck in the traveller's belt.

ST. JAMES'S PARK

UNTIL it was enclosed by Henry VIII, St. James's Park was a huge, undrained field belonging to the hospital, afterwards St. James's Palace. Charles II had the Park replanted, and beautified—according to the fashion and taste of the time. One of Charles's advisers was Le Notre, architect of the groves and grottos of Versailles.

The Park remained much as Charles planned it, during the succeeding reigns of William and Mary and Anne. The account for Charles's improvements, signed by the King, included 670 loads of gravel for roadmaking, at 12d. a load ; 1023 loads at 8d. a load ; and 400 bolts of reeds for the Decoy (not seen in our picture map) in which Charles kept ducks and various water-fowl.

Pepys refers in his diaries of 1660 to the making of a " river through the Park," and of 300 men, " every day employed in his majesty's worke. in making the River in St. James's Park and repairing Whitehall." Other writers called it a canal. It united several pools and springs into one sheet of water, 28 feet broad, 100 feet long. A subterranean channel connected it with the Thames so that it could be replenished therefrom.

Of the formal design of the tree-planting, seen in this coloured print of Queen Anne's time, Ned Ward, in his *London Spy*, writes of " a long lime-walk, where both Art and Nature had carefully preserved the trees in such exact proportion to each other that a man would guess by their appearance they all aspire in height and spread in breadth to just the same dimensions, and confine their leaves and branches to an equal number." Ward (1667–1731) was a humorist and writer of coarse, satirical verse. Still, he was contemporary, and his descriptions of London life are first-hand.

He tells of " pensive lovers whispering their affections to their mistresses, and breathing out despairing sighs of their

Continued on page facing 33

Her Maj.ties Royal P...

To Her most Serene and most Sacred Majesty ANNE by y...

1 Queens Palace.   2 St James' Chapell.   3 Duke of Marlboroughs House.   4 The Lord Godolphin's House.   5 The Canal.   6 The Mall.

rk of St. James's

Grace of God QUEEN of Great Britain France & Ireland &c.

7. The Horse Guards. 8. The Banquetting House. 9. Whitehal. 10. The Admiralty House. 11. Spring Garden. 12. Charing-Cross.

ST. JAMES'S PARK

Continued from page facing 32

tender happiness," under the regular and pleasant shade of these formal avenues.

By Rosamond's Pond, a square sheet of water at the west end of the long water, was a knot of elms, " and commodious seats for the tired ambulators to refresh their pedestals. Here a parcel of old, worn-out Cavaliers were conning over the Civil Wars, and looking back into the history of their past lives."

Such seats were abandoned to the lower orders, according to Jacob Larwood, historian of the royal parks. Those at the end of the Mall were pretty full between the hours of 12 and 3 o'clock " with knots of sage politicians."

Larwood pictures the Mall peopled with fine ladies, " patched and painted, hooped and farthingaled, adorned with fly-caps, top-knots, tight-laced bodices, laced aprons, and flounced petti-coats, for the display of which the gown was gathered in folds behind." The pretty fellows who ogled and flirted with them were decked out in square-tailed silk or velvet coats, of all colours of the rainbow. They " tripped mincingly upon their toes humming a tune, with a small hat on the top of a wheelbarrowful of periwig, covered with a bushel of powder. Their sword-knots trailed almost on the ground, and their canes dangled from the fifth button. This splendid *ensemble* was terminated with pearl-coloured stockings, and shoes with red heels."

The mansion at the west end of the canal is Buckingham House, built in 1705 for the Duke of that name. It was bought by George III in 1762, and all his children, except George IV, were born here. George IV, who finally re-arranged the Park much as it is to-day, had Buckingham House re-built from the designs of John Nash about 1825. In 1847 Edward Blore designed the long east wing, facing the Park, converting the whole into a quadrangle round an inner courtyard : in 1913, Blore's wing was replaced by the present dignified front designed by Sir Aston Webb.

Top : **State carriage in carved wood with the Royal Arms of King George II. 1760-1770.**

By courtesy of the Victoria and Albert Museum.

Above : **An eighteenth-century doll's house, dated 1750.**

By courtesy of the London Museum.

Right : **A mid-eighteenth-century sedan chair.**

By courtesy of the Victoria and Albert Museum.

33

FLEET PRISON AND ITS MARRIAGES

THE Temple as we knew it before Hitler wrought havoc there had not altered much in two hundred years. One addition was Middle Temple Library, opened in 1861; another change was the rebuilding in 1869 of Inner Temple Hall and Library.

Temple Bar, a gateway of Portland stone separating the Strand from Fleet Street, is close to the border of the Section. It remained in position until 1878. It was an extra-mural barrier and marked the limit here of the City liberties outside the walls, as does the Memorial in its place to-day. The corresponding City gate was Ludgate, which stood just west of St. Martin Ludgate, on what we know as Ludgate Hill. As the map shows, it was Ludgate Street in 1746.

There were iron spikes above the centre pediment of Temple Bar, on which were placed the heads, and sometimes the limbs, of persons executed for treason. Walpole saw, in August 1746, "the new heads at Temple Bar, where people make a trade of letting spy-glasses at a halfpenny a look." The heads were probably those of the Jacobites Towneley, Fletcher, and others, the last to be thus exhibited. Towneley's head was secretly removed one night for burial in the family vault; the others remained until they fell or were blown down.

Visiting the Poets' Corner in Westminster Abbey with Goldsmith, Dr. Johnson quoted Ovid: "*Forsitan et nostrum nomen miscebitur istis*" (Perhaps too my name will be joined to theirs). "When we got to the Temple Bar," Dr. Johnson related to Boswell, "Goldsmith stopped me, pointed to the heads upon it and slily whispered me: '*Forsitan et nostrum nomen miscebitur istis.*'"

One Serjeants' Inn will be noticed in Chancery Lane, another off Fleet Street. The latter, demolished by Hitler, had ceased to be an Inn of Court at the date of our map; the former continued as such until the dissolution of the Society of Serjeants' Inn in 1876. The Serjeant's was the highest degree in Common Law: he wore a coif—a circular black patch—on the top of his wig to distinguish him in Court.

Blue Ball Court, off Salisbury Square, is now St. Bride's Passage. Here was the printing office and warehouse of Samuel Richardson, printer and novelist, who lived in the Square. His sentimental novel *Pamela; or Virtue Rewarded* was written in Salisbury Square in 1740. At the time of our map his seven-volume *Clarissa; or the History of a Young Lady* was appearing, two volumes at a time.

St. Bride's Church, one of Wren's architectural glories, which Hitler's fire-bombs completely gutted, has its old name of St. Bridget's on our map. It was finished in 1703. Richardson was buried in the church.

Samuel Richardson

Bridewell was a famous house of detention where vagrants, harlots, and idle and disobedient apprentices, sentenced to short terms of imprisonment, beat hemp and picked oakum for their sins. The prison and its chapel were demolished during 1863–71.

Farringdon Street and New Bridge Street have taken the place of the Fleet Ditch, now a sewer which discharges into the Thames under Blackfriars Bridge. The bridge over the Ditch at the bottom of Fleet Street is now Ludgate Circus. These improvements came in 1765 when the first Blackfriars Bridge was built.

The Fleet Prison of our map was that built anew after the Great Fire. It had been better regulated after the enquiry of 1729, which Hogarth depicted in a famous picture. The prisoners were debtors, bankrupts, and persons charged with contempt of court. Under certain conditions debtors were allowed to live outside the prison, within a specified area known as the Liberties or Rules of the Fleet. Thousands of irregular marriages were contracted without licence in the Liberties. Register books of Fleet marriages are preserved at Somerset House, as collateral evidence of such marriages.

Ludgate, also a prison for debtors as well as a gate of the City walls, remained until 1762. Over the doorway of parish schools beside the church of St. Dunstan in the West, Fleet Street, is a marble statue of Queen Elizabeth, holding sceptre and orb, that originally stood in a niche on the west side of Ludgate.

Newgate Market, for meat, disappeared in 1800, and Paternoster Square, since destroyed by Hitler, brought publishers' and booksellers' premises where butchers' shops and shambles had been.

St. Paul's Churchyard was more spacious than it is to-day, and Cannon Street had not taken the place of Distaff Lane. St. Paul's School, third building on the site, was standing on the east side of the churchyard. It was removed to West Kensington in 1880.

Blackfriars Bridge now spans the river from the Fleet Ditch to Marygold Stairs, and Blackfriars Road has been made in a straight line due south to St. George's Circus (just beyond the border of this Section). From 1769 to 1829 it was known as Great Surrey Street. Christ Church, shown in Green Walk, is now in Blackfriars Road. The present church was built 1738–41, but was enlarged in 1816, and a chancel was added in 1870.

In the right-hand bottom corner are Lombard Street, Mint Square, and a part of Mint Street. There had been " a Mint of Coinage there kept for the King " in Henry VIII's reign, according to Stow. At the time of our map this area had long been a sanctuary for insolvent debtors, also a harbour for thieves and lawless persons of all descriptions: thus, Lombard Street was originally a cant name, derived from the fraudulent debtors living there. Mat of the Mint was one of Macheath's gang in *The Beggar's Opera*.

A portion of Mint Street remains to-day, but the whole area of ill-fame was cleared in 1877.

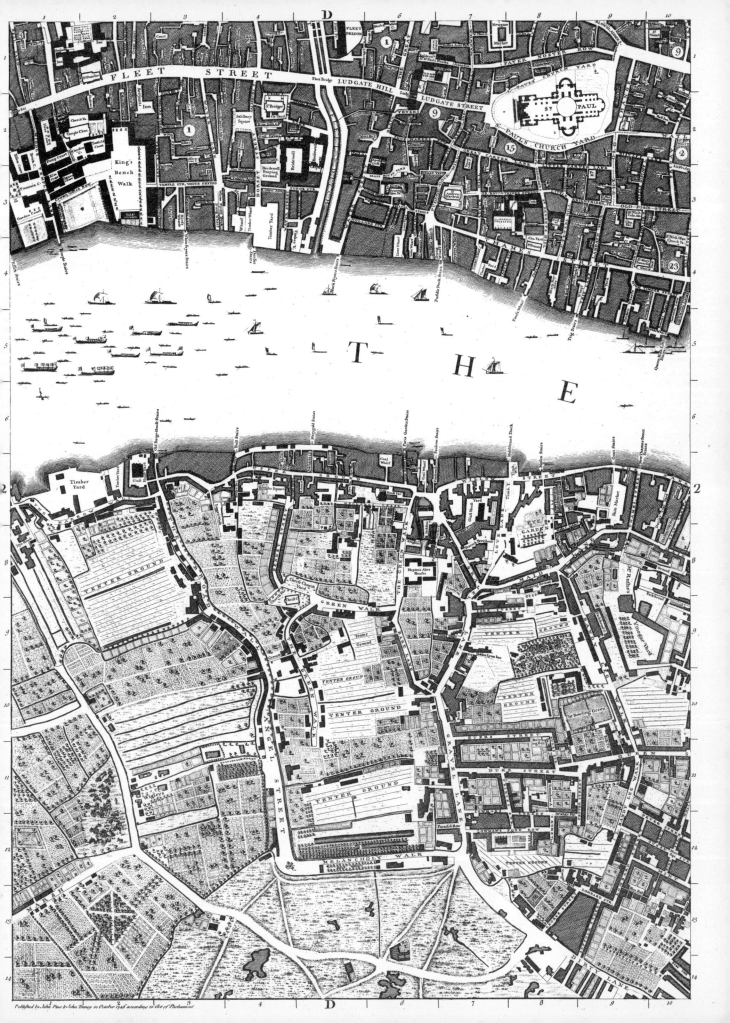

FLEET STREET

FLEET PRISON

Newgate Market

LUDGATE HILL

Fleet Bridge

LUDGATE STREET

PATER NOSTER ROW

St BRIDE'S

Salisbury Square

ST PAUL'S CHURCH YARD

St PAUL

King's Bench Walk

Bridewell Burying Ground

Bridewell

TEMPLE STR. WHITE FRYERS

DORSET STREET

Timber Yard

Timber Wharf

Wharf

THE

Timber Yard

Timber Yard

Old Barge-House Stairs

Coal Wharf

Skin Market

SCROTUS SQUARE

House Yard

TENTER GROUND

Christ Church Yard

GREEN WALK

Hopkins Alms Houses

THE GREEN WALK

Tenter Ground

TENTER GROUND

Golden Lyon Inn

TENTER GROUND

The Bowling Green

DUKE STREET

ANGEL STREET

TENTER GROUND

Paradise Row

GRAVEL LANE

TENTER GROUND

MELANCHOLY WALK

Published by John Pine & John Tinney in October 1746 according to Act of Parliament

FALSTAFF'S NIGHT AT THE WINDMILL

ON a level with the word FIELDS on this Section is a windmill. It brings to mind a supposed reminiscence of Shallow and Falstaff, in Part Two of *Henry IV*. "O, Sir John," cries the vainglorious justice, "do you remember since we lay all night in the windmill in St. George's Fields?" To which the fat knight, playing up to him, replies, "No more of that, good master Shallow; no more of that." "Ha," boasts Shallow, "it was a merry night."

One would like to think this was the windmill Shakespeare had in mind. St. George's Fields were a resort of Londoners, and right up to 1768 local people had right of common and pasturage. In Shakespeare's time, and long after, the Fields were used for musters of soldiers, volunteers and train bands, and for meetings of trades to air their grievances.

In the second part of *Henry VI*, Act v, Scene 1, Richard Plantagenet, Duke of York, says to his army, ". . . disperse yourselves. Meet me to-morrow in St. George's Field." Though the suggestion is a particular field, which could be anywhere, it is not unlikely that Shakespeare was again thinking of this common land.

There was an historic muster here in 1780, when the "No Popery" rioters gathered under Lord George Gordon. Their assembly point is known. It was at the place where Bethlehem Hospital (now the Imperial War Museum) stands, immediately north of the Dog and Duck. The latter is shown on our map in Lambeth Road.

Eight busy main roads now run over this once-common land. Six of them meet at St. George's Circus, which is about the middle of the word FIELDS on our map. The six roads are Blackfriars Road, running due north; then, reading clock-wise on a modern map, Borough Road, London Road, Lambeth Road (not that on our map, for that is now St. George's Road, swinging north-west well above the Dog and Duck), Westminster Bridge Road, and Waterloo Road.

On the west side of our map, near the top, can be seen the unnamed beginning of Kennington Road, which now runs down to meet Kennington Lane, and continues beyond the latter due south.

The Dog and Duck was enjoying a new prosperity at the time our map was made. It had been a small public-house, with a pond attached in which the barbarous "sport" of duck-hunting was practised. The amusement consisted in the duck diving among the reeds with the dog in pursuit.

When Bethlehem Hospital was built in 1815, the old stone sign of the Dog and Duck was embedded in its garden wall. The sign is in two divisions. One bears the date 1716 and the device of the City Corporation's Bridge House Estate, of which this land was a part. The other half shows a spaniel of sorts, sitting on its haunches, with a duck in its mouth.

What brought prosperity to the Dog and Duck was a circus, set up in the fields opposite the inn. Out of the profits of much-increased custom, the landlord extended his premises and built up a pleasure resort. Presently a mineral spring, always a good draw, was discovered, and doctors pronounced its waters medicinal. By 1771 no less a person than Dr. Johnson was recommending, to Mrs Thrale, the waters of St. George's Spa.

Turn your eyes now to the little triangle of land in Newington Butts. You will hardly recognise the northern point of this triangle as the congested cross-roads at the Elephant and Castle, but such it is. The other long side of the triangle is Walworth Road, which to-day becomes Camberwell Road farther south.

All but one of the thoroughfares converging on the Elephant and Castle (the celebrated old tavern had not appeared when our map was drawn) can be traced, though London Road, between Lambeth (i.e. St. George's) Road and Newington Causeway (northern extension of Newington Butts) is seen as a footpath across the fields. The one thoroughfare at the Elephant not on our map is New Kent Road, which is almost an extension eastwards of its Lambeth Road.

Spurgeon's, or the Metropolitan Tabernacle, in Newington Butts, was gutted by Hitler's fire-bombs in 1941. In the place where its ruined shell now stands, picturesque alms-houses of the Fishmongers' Company flourished two hundred years ago. They were Gothic structures with mullioned windows, and had gardens about them bounded by low walls. Founded in 1618, they were moved to new premises on Wandsworth Common in 1851.

A little lower on our map is St. Mary's Church, which had just been constructed on the site of a sixteenth-century church. There was still a third St. Mary's to come before the present edifice opposite Kennington Oval station succeeded it in 1877. Some time after this, when the 1793 church had been demolished, the present church of St. Gabriel was erected where the original St. Mary's had stood.

One tiny street on our map, called Peacock Lane, survives to-day—as Peacock Street. It is at the junction of Kennington Lane, Newington Butts and Road to Clapham (now Kennington Park Road).

The sign of "The Dog and Duck"

Published by John Pine & John Tinney in October 1746 according to Act of Parliament

St GEORGES

FIELDS

LAMBETH ROAD

Dog and Duck

Windmill

BLACK

BUTTS

NEWINGTON

ROAD TO CAMBERWELL

Rowington Church Yard

LANE

ROAD TO CLAPHAM

LANE

D

D

A. PL
the CI
LONDON AND W
and BOR
SOUTH
with
CONTIGUOUS

From an actual SURVE
Land-Surveyor, *and* En
BLUEMANTLE Purfuiv
Engraver
To His

This Work was
1737. and Publ
1746. according
ment, by IOHN
Golden Head a
ton House Picca
TINNEY at the
Street LONDON
are to

LAUGHING AT BEDLAM'S LUNATICS

THE close detail in this Section deserves study with a magnifying glass. One wonders how the mapmakers outlined so many hundreds of tiny courts, alleys, nooks and crannies. Far-reaching changes have swept away these rabbit warrens, and to-day they are much more open. On the other hand, most of the big open spaces have been built up.

The Artillery Ground remains, however, and beside it Finsbury Square on what was Upper Moor Fields. Tindall's Burying Ground is now Bunhill Fields : little Hoxton Square still exists, also Charles Square ; and the Technical School of the Haberdashers—in place of Aske's Hospital, shown on our map north of Petfield (Pitfield) Street—has its gardens.

Major changes are the introduction of City Road, opened in 1761, which enters this Section almost diagonally from the left-hand top corner to a point north of the turnpike in Old Street, then takes the place of Royal Row. Old Street, built upon a Roman road, is the broad thoroughfare running across the Section to Hoxton in the right-hand top corner.

Finsbury by Moorfields on our map is Finsbury Pavement, but the modern street known as Moorgate begins north of the postern in the street called London Wall, and continues south, parallel with Coleman Street. The postern called Moorgate was not of Roman origin like other entrances to the walled City, but was an opening made in the wall by Thomas Falconer, Mayor in 1415, " for the ease of the citizens to walk that way upon causeys towards Isledon and Hoxton," says Stow. The gate was demolished in 1762.

Cripplegate, at the west end of London Wall, was also a postern, but a much older one. Stow, who dates it from 1099, quotes the supposition that it was so called from cripples begging there ; later authorities say the name is Angle-Saxon for a covered way. It was pulled down in 1760. Bishopsgate, at the other end of London Wall, was removed a few years later.

The Bethlem Hospital, shown in London Wall, was the second Bedlam, completed in 1676, and described by Evelyn as " magnificently built and most sweetly placed in Moorfields." It succeeded the old Priory of Bethlehem in Bishopsgate, founded in 1246 and given by Henry VIII to the City of London for conversion into a hospital for lunatics. Like its predecessor, the Bedlam of our period was open

as an exhibition, payment being made for admission to see the wretched folk imprisoned there as lunatics, and to laugh at their antics. All whose nervous organisms were in any way abnormal were thrust into Bedlam, truly a haunt of tragedy. Hogarth pictures the scene in " A Rake's Progress." Not until 1770 did the authorities decide that sight-seers aggravated the mental disorders of patients.

South Front of Bedlam

William Cowper, the poet, wrote in 1784 of his visit : " In the days when Bedlam was open to the cruel curiosity of holiday ramblers. . . . Though a boy, I was not altogether insensible to the misery of the poor captives, nor destitute of feeling for them. But the madness of some of them has such a humorous air, and displayed itself in so many whimsical freaks, that it was impossible not to be entertained at the same time that I was angry with myself for being so." Bethlem Hospital remained in London Wall until 1815.

Another great change was the advent of Broad Street and Liverpool Street stations, side by side, and parallel with Bishopsgate Street. Liverpool Street itself is Old Bethlem on our map : widened and largely rebuilt, and in 1829 renamed in honour of Lord Liverpool, Prime Minister, who had just died. The two termini occupy a part of Moorfields, and all of Bethlem Burying Ground. Liverpool Street station spreads eastwards to Bishopsgate Street.

Guildhall, between Aldermanbury and Bassinghall Street, had a smaller and better-looking front at the time of our map, the " large arch of entrance sustained at the sides by columns having enriched spandrels with shells containing the arms of England and of Edward the Confessor." Half a dozen symbolical figures stood in niches, " their attitudes easy and elegant and the sculpture good." The present front, by George Dance, was substituted in 1789.

Blackwell Hall was then standing opposite St. Lawrence Jewry, remaining there until 1820. It was a weekly market for woollen cloths, established in the thirteenth century.

The street called The Curtain, running north from the east end of Worship Street, is now Curtain Road. It got its name from a fortification of the outworks of old London Wall. Here, Stow records, " are builded two publique-houses for the acting and shewe of comedies, tragedies, and histories for recreation. Whereof one is called the Courtein, the other the Theatre, both standing on the south-west side towards the field."

It cannot be said with complete certainty where these primitive playhouses stood, except that they were in Holywell Priory. At the Curtain *Romeo and Juliet* was performed, probably for the first time, in 1598. In the same year the Theatre was pulled down, and the timber was carried to Southwark and there used in construction of the Globe Theatre.

St. Agnes le Claire in Old Street, opposite the bottom of Pitfield Street, was a celebrated well. " Somewhat north from Holywell is one other well, curved square with stone, and is called Dame Annis the clear, and not far from it, but somewhat west, is also one other clear water called Perilous pond, because divers youths by swimming therein have been drowned."

Thus the inimitable Stow. At the time of our map the bathing pond had been enclosed and its depth reduced. Its name was now Peerless Pond, and a larger pond nearby had been enclosed for fishing. Swimmers and anglers rejoiced in them until 1805, when the ponds were drained and the area was built over.

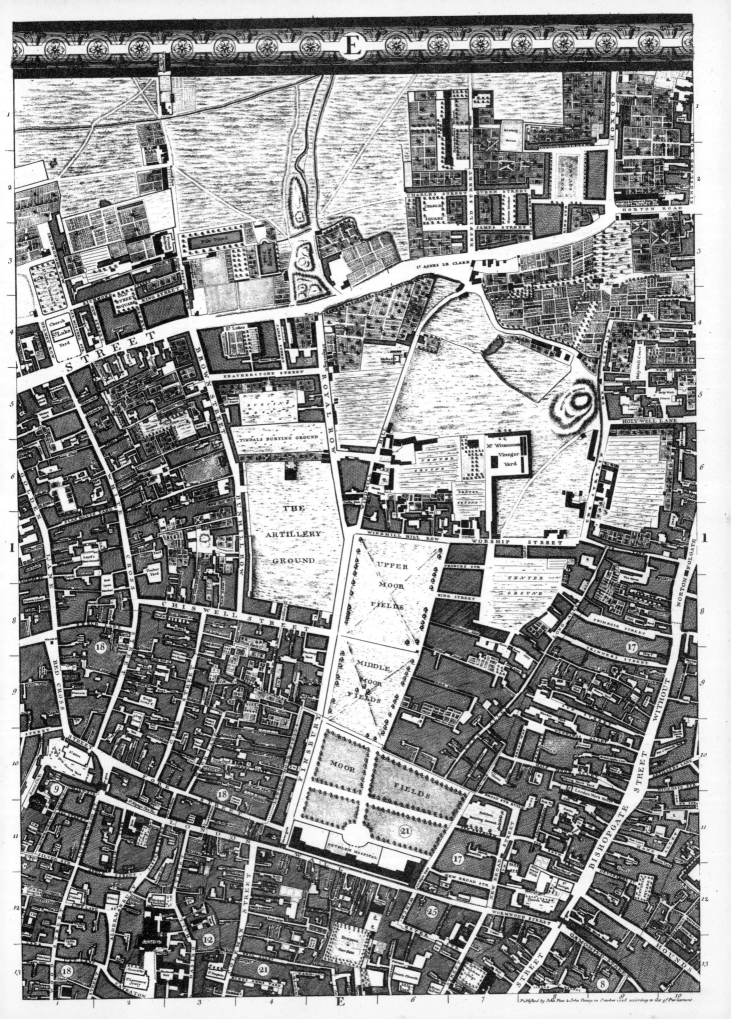

Published by John Pine & John Tinney in October 1748 according to Act of Parliament

THOMAS GUY, THE FRUGAL BOOKSELLER

THIS Section of our map covers the heart of London—three-quarters of a mile of the Thames, with London Bridge in the centre, with the Mansion House, the Bank of England, Leadenhall Market, and a maze of business streets north of the bridge ; with Southwark, Bermondsey Street, and the great hospitals, St. Thomas's and Guy's, in streets leading out of The Borough.

This London Bridge, built between 1176 and 1209, was 200 feet east of the present structure. It had twenty narrow arches, a drawbridge for larger vessels, and on it a chapel, also shops and houses so that it was like a continuous street.

Fire swept this bridge in 1633, and houses then burned were not rebuilt : the last of those remaining were removed in 1757. The old bridge was constantly in need of repair, and the weight of the houses was too much for it.

The waterway was obstructed by the narrowness of the arches : in some of them were corn mills and waterworks. There was such a rush of water through those left open that " shooting the bridge " in a boat, for which oars had to be shipped, was perilous.

A feature of the river banks at this time was the large number of stairs on both sides of the water. In this three-quarter - mile stretch there are twenty-one stairs. They remind us how much of a highway the river was for London citizens, when there was no other substitute for present-day buses, trams, and underground trains, and when there were very few public vehicles on the streets for passenger hire.

The Mansion House looks as if it had been moved. This is because the open space before the Royal Exchange had not been created. A hundred years later Queen Victoria Street was to come up from the newly constructed Victoria Embankment, cutting through Queen Street and Bucklersbury. The Royal Exchange at the date of our map.was the second building on the present site. It had a clock tower on the Cornhill front, and faced that way.

Daniel Defoe, writing about London at this time, thought this Royal Exchange the greatest and finest in the world. It was a market containing dozens of small shops. Said Defoe : " 'Tis observable that tho' this Exchange cost the citizens an immense sum of money (actually £58,962) . . . yet the rent or income fully answered the interest of the money laid out in the building of it ; whether it does so still or not, I will not say, the trade for millinery goods which was so great . . . being since scattered and removed, and the shops, many of them, left empty."

Leadenhall, London's oldest market, had three sections : in the Hide market beef was sold, also hides on certain days ; the Green market was for veal, mutton, and lamb ; the Herb market was for vegetables, roots, and fruit. Poulterers, pre-eminent here—as they are to-day—occupied tenements surrounding and among these three markets.

Leadenhall had for its neighbour in Leadenhall Street, East India House, premises of the largest and most magnificent company in the world. Horace Walpole termed the Company " sovereigns of Bengal." For two and a half centuries it governed India from this place, and not until after the Mutiny was that sovereignty transferred to the Crown. Charles Lamb was a clerk in East India House for thirty-three years.

The still more widely influential transactions of Lloyd's corporation of marine underwriters are carried on now in a great modern building on the same site to-day. It is the world's centre of marine insurance, and its influence is felt in every port, on every ocean, and on the great lakes of North America.

Off The Borough, south side of the river, you will notice St. Thomas's Hospital. It had been there since its foundation in 1213 by the Prior of Bermondsey. It was bought by the citizens of London in 1552, and in 1701–6 was rebuilt by public subscription. The hospital moved to its present place along the river beside Westminster Bridge in 1871, to make way for London Bridge station of the Southern Railway.

Close to St. Thomas's is another great hospital, Guy's, which to-day is still on this, its original, site. At the time this map was made the hospital had been open twenty-one years. Thomas Guy, its founder, had lived to see the roof put on. He was a bookseller who started in business at the corner of Cornhill and Lombard Street, sold a great many Bibles, accumulated money, and invested it in Government securities. He was a bachelor of frugal habits who lunched on his shop counter with an old newspaper for table-cloth. Largely by the timely selling of his South Sea shares he became something near to a millionaire, and he left more than £100,000 to relatives and friends, as well as the money for the hospital which bears his name.

On the other side of the Borough high street is an open space—at the corner of Red Cross Street (now Red Cross Way) and Castle Street—described on the map as Tenter Ground. There is a larger one in Snows Fields between Bermondsey Street and The Borough. A tenter is a large wooden frame used in the manufacture of cloth to stretch out the pieces of stuff so that they dry or set evenly and square without shrinking. So you get the expression " on tenter hooks," meaning to be in suspense.

These tenter grounds, to be found in many other places in London at this time, are evidence that cloth of one sort or another was manufactured widely. As an industry it was later to leave London for Lancashire and Yorkshire and the West country.

Tooley Street, beginning near the south foot of London Bridge, is a curious corruption of St. Olave's Street, of which it appears in our map as a continuation. It derives its name from the church of St. Olave's. At various times it has been written Towllys, Tulies, and Soules. It used to be famous for the story of " the three tailors of Tooley Street," who called a meeting for redress of popular grievances, and began their petition to Parliament, " We, the people of England . . ."

ROAD OF PILGRIMS, WARRIORS, REBELS

HAPPENINGS of great moment in history passed to and from the City via Kent Street and Old Kent Road, which dominate this Section of our map.

First the Roman invader—for this route was that of Watling Street; then, in the reverse direction, many thousands of pilgrims (including Chaucer's in 1385) making their way to the shrine of Thomas à Becket at Canterbury; next (1385) the Black Prince with the captive French King, returning to London from Poictiers; then (1450) Jack Cade with his 20,000 Kentish men; Sir Thomas Wyat (1554) and his followers, marching to find London Bridge closed against him; and (1660) Charles II, returning to the re-established monarchy in colourful, triumphant State.

"What long lines of conquest and devotion, of turmoil and rebellion, of victory, gorgeous pageantry, and grim death," says John Timbs, "have poured through this narrow inlet of old London!"

But Smollett records of Kent Street that this was a most disgraceful entrance to an opulent city, and what he wrote of it in 1766 was doubtless true at the time of our map: "A foreigner, in passing through this beggarly and ruinous suburb, conceives such an idea of misery and meanness as all the wealth and magnificence of London and Westminster are afterwards unable to destroy."

And, as our map records, Old Kent Road ran through fields and hedgerows two hundred years ago, with no other habitation a mile beyond London Bridge than occasional farm-houses and wayside inns.

Kent Street is now Tabard Street, so named after the great inn whence Chaucer starts his company on their pilgrimage. Tabard Street was by-passed in 1809 by Great Dover Street which enters Old Kent Road a little to the north of One Mile Stone.

Bermondsey Abbey

This mile-stone, a rugged old cube, was still to be seen until January 1947 on the pavement beside 35 Old Kent Road: it bore an iron plate before the last war recording that it is one mile thence to London Bridge, and 14 miles to Dartford.

Near the mile-stone, New Kent Road turns due west, and Tower Bridge Road runs in a north-easterly direction to King's (now Grange) Road. Thence it curves round the east side of Bermondsey Church Yard on our map, and continues to the top corner of the Section.

The unnamed building below the mile-stone, and on the same side of the highway, is probably the wayside inn which preceded the Bricklayers' Arms. The Southern Railway goods station of that name begins considerably south of the mile-stone, at the point where an inn called the White Hart is shown on our map. The line of hedge running up to Pages Walk is now a street known by that name also, and is a connection between King's (Grange) Road and Old Kent Road.

Just as Old Kent Road was the route from Dover and the Continent, so Bricklayers' Arms station, when first opened here, was the terminus for arrivals and departures of distinguished visitors from abroad—until Charing Cross station was established.

One more item of interest near the mile-stone is the Loke, or Lock hospital: from the fourteenth century there had been a lazar house, or hospital for lepers, here. The southern end of Great Dover Street now occupies the site.

Long Lane, at the top of the Section, is probably as old as Kent Street, for it was a common way, from the earliest times, to that place of great resort, Bermondsey Abbey. This monastery of the Cluniac order, founded in 1082, had political significance as a sanctuary, and here died Henry V's Queen, Catherine, in 1437, and Edward IV's widow, Elizabeth, in 1492.

The Abbey occupied the ground between Grange Walk and Long Walk. Its east gate was in Grange Walk until 1760, and the great gate-house was nearly entire until 1806, when Abbey Street and Bermondsey Square took the place of Long Walk.

At the time of our map, however, there existed a neglected quadrangle called King John's Court, from some tradition of this monarch's visit to the Abbey. The form and antiquity of the windows in this court showed they had been a part of the monastery buildings.

St. Mary Magdalene alone remains of the great religious holding. It was built in 1680 by the priors of the Abbey, on the site of an earlier foundation, for the use of their tenantry. There have been many alterations and additions to the church. Among its plate is a beautiful silver-gilt dish of about 1400, when the Abbey flourished. It is engraved in the middle with the kneeling figure of a knight in armour, on whose head a lady is placing a tilting-helm. A horse, trees, and a mediaeval building are in the background.

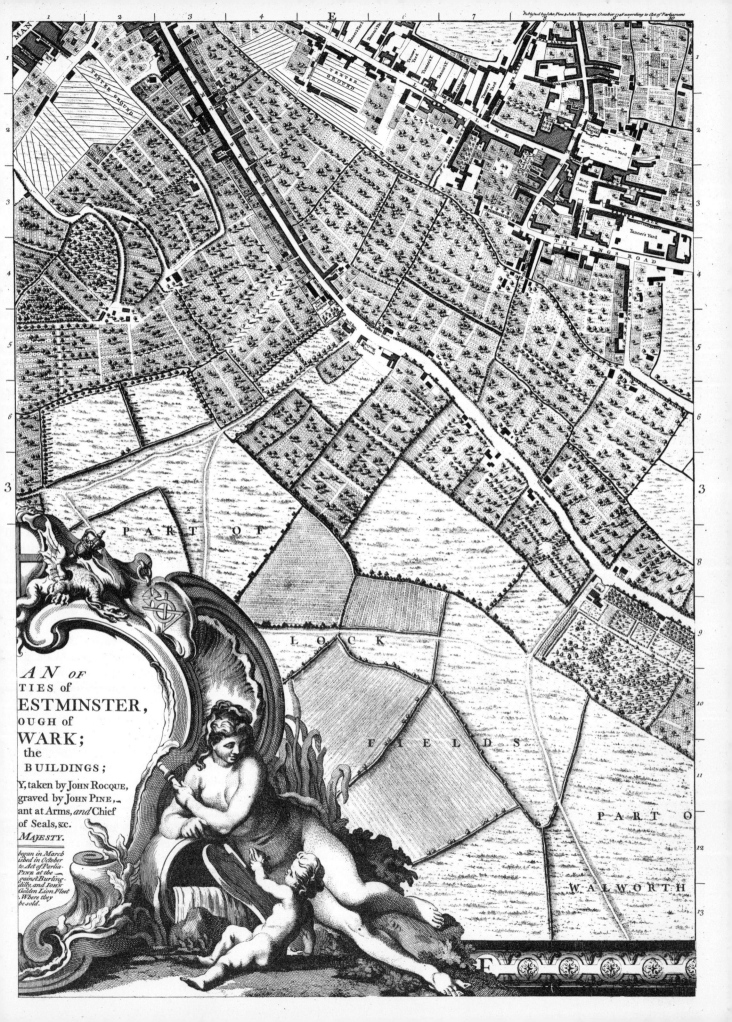

TENTER GROUND

TENTER GROUND

TENTER GROUND

LONG LANE

Bermondsey Church Yard

King James's Court

Tanners Yard

THE KINGS ROAD

School

WALWORTH

PART OF

LOCK

FIELDS

PART O

WALWORTH

AN OF
TIES of
ESTMINSTER,
OUGH of
WARK;
the
BUILDINGS;
Y, taken by JOHN ROCQUE,
graved by JOHN PINE,
ant at Arms, and Chief
of Seals, &c.
MAJESTY.

begun in March
ibed in October
to Act of Parlia
PINE at the
gainst Burling
dilly, and JOHN
Golden Lion Fleet
. Where they
be sold.

Published by John Pine & John Tinney, en October 1746 according to Act of Parliament

BLIND BEGGAR OF BETHNAL GREEN

SINCE our map was made, three main thoroughfares have grown into this Section, which embraces a portion of Bethnal Green, and lesser portions of Shoreditch and Whitechapel, Stepney.

The thoroughfares are : (a) in the north, Hackney Road, curving away in a north-easterly direction from St. Leonard's Church, Shoreditch, partly replacing Crabtree Lane ; (b) Bethnal Green Road, leaving Shoreditch High Street at Swan Yard, by Anchor Street, and swinging up to New Cock Lane, Church Street, and along the road not named on our map ; (c) Commercial Road, beginning west of Church Lane in Whitechapel High Street, and running east almost parallel with the bottom of the Section.

From where Commercial Road joins Whitechapel High Street, a thoroughfare scarcely less important than these, namely, Commercial Street, from the other side links the High Streets of Whitechapel and Shoreditch at about the first letter 'h' in Shoreditch. There is also a portion of Kingsland Road : it runs due north from St. Leonard's Church.

Brick Lane on our map is now extended north to Virginia Row (Road), so that it is nearly three-quarters of a mile long. Benjamin Truman's brewery flourished two hundred years ago in Brick Lane—as does its successor to-day—between Quaker Street and Brown's Lane. The latter is now Hanbury Street.

When Princess Augusta, later Duchess of Brunswick, was born in 1737, Frederick, Prince of Wales, her father, ordered a bonfire outside Carlton House, with free Royal beer for the crowd. The beer proved to be of inferior quality and caused a small riot ; so the Prince ordered a bonfire for the following night. This time Benjamin Truman supplied the beer, and it was apparently more satisfactory.

Changes just as great as those effected by the development of main thoroughfares were brought about by the building of the Eastern Counties Railway, across the centre of this Section at St. John's Street and Phoenix Street, to what is now Bishopsgate Goods Station of the L.N.E.R. Erected in 1843, this station was the terminus of the railway until the line was extended to Liverpool Street.

The parish of Spitalfields has changed much, largely through the growth of its ancient market into one of the largest and most modern distribution centres in the world for fruit, flowers, and vegetables.

At the time of our map Spitalfields was a centre for the weaving of silks and velvets. In several small streets around Spital Square and Market, Crispin Street, and Christ Church, much-decayed little houses of the weavers remain. They can be recognised by the long windows, weather-boarded, built into the roofs to utilise the daylight at their looms. Many thousands of looms were operated in such homes by the wretchedly-paid weavers and throwsters. They were mostly English ; but many, like their employers, were of French origin and descended from Hugenot refugees. Petticoat Lane, in the left-hand bottom corner of this Section, was inhabited at its northern end by silk weavers two hundred years ago.

Strype Yard, a narrow turning on the right in Petticoat Lane, is named after the antiquary's father. It is now Strype Street, and a stone recently set in the face of a house at the foot of what was the yard, commemorate's Strype's birth, " in a fair large house with a good garden before it." It must have been very different from the humble building on the site to-day.

Christ Church, Spitalfields, was built in 1723–29, a massive edifice of stone, with a tower 30 feet higher than the Monument. There is now a school on the Brick Lane side of its drab, neglected churchyard.

In Cock Lane, near St. Leonard's Church, Shoreditch, a granddaughter of John Milton was living when our map was drawn. In his " Life " of the poet, Dr. Johnson tells : " She married Thomas Foster, a weaver in Spitalfields, and had seven children, who all died. She kept a petty grocer's or chandler's shop in Pelham Street (off Brick Lane). . . . She knew little of her grandfather, and that little was not good. In 1750, April 5, *Comus* was played for her benefit." The benefit produced £150, but Mrs. Foster died in poverty at Islington four years later.

The site of London Hospital is beside the east border of the Section, on the south side of White Chapel Street. Behind it, leading away to Stepney Church, is Oxford Street, an extension of White Chapel Field Gate which on our map does lead into fields. The Hospital was in Prescot Street, Goodman's Fields (south of this Section) at the time of our map ; the building of the present premises began in 1752.

St. Matthew Church stands alone in a spacious churchyard, almost surrounded by fields. Built in 1740, it was burned out in December 1859, when during a hard frost the water froze as it was poured on the fire. Handsomely rebuilt after the fire, it was again gutted by Hitler's bombs.

Its beadle uses an old staff, the silver-gilt head of which presents the legend of the Blind Beggar of Bethnal Green. Old ballads, including Percy's " Reliques of Ancient English Poetry," identify the Beggar as Henry, son and heir of Simon of Montfort, left for dead on the battlefield of Evesham. If in truth he were Henry of Montfort, then some other knight was buried with Simon at Evesham as his son Henry.

The ballad tells that he was discovered by a baron's daughter who nursed him to recovery and married him. He assumes the garb and semblance of a beggar as a disguise from his enemies. He has a beautiful daughter who is courted simultaneously by four suitors. All withdraw on learning her father is a beggar, except one true knight. The Beggar gives her £100 for a wedding gown, and £3000 for a dower, and at the wedding feast casts his disguise—and they all lived happily ever after, no doubt !

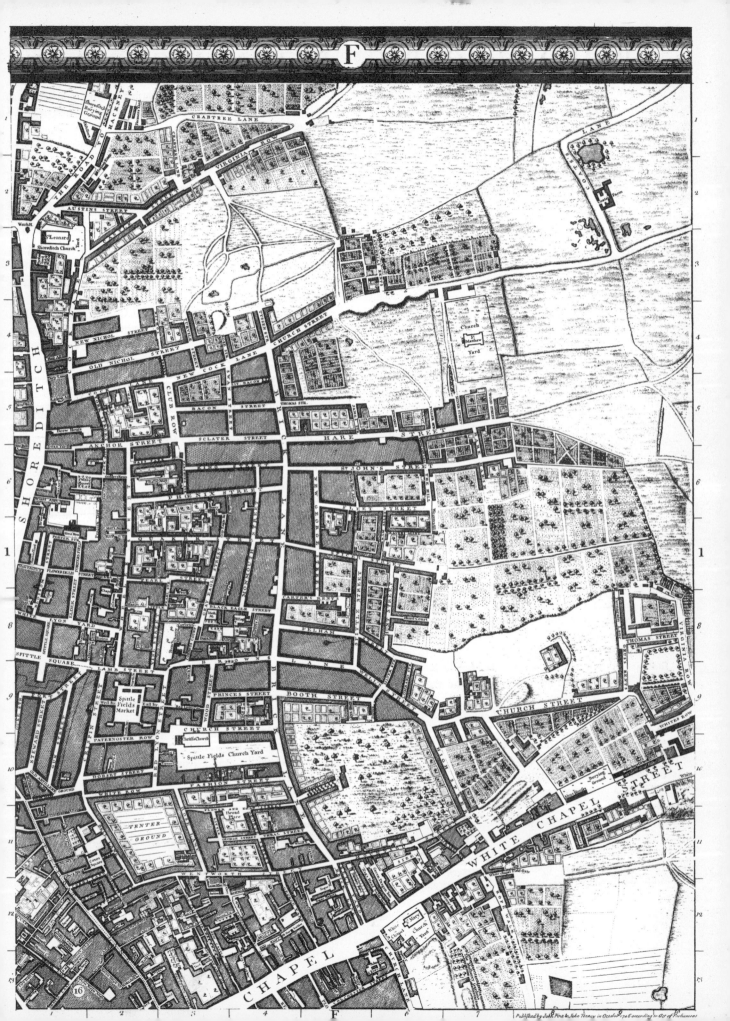

CRABTREE LANE

Shoreditch Burying Ground

THE ROAD TO HACKNEY

VIRGINIA ROW

VIRGINIA STREET

AUSTINS STREET

WatchH.

St Leonard Shoreditch Church

LANE

Farm

Church St Matthew Yard

NEW NICHOL STREET

OLD NICHOL STREET

CHURCH STREET

NEW COCK LANE

CLUB ROW

SHOREDITCH

Brew House

BACON STREET

THOMAS STR.

ANCHOR STREET

SCLATER STREET

HARE STREET

St JOHN'S STREET

PHENIX STREET

NEW GEORGE STREET

BLACK EAGLE STREET

CARTERS RENTS

PELHAM

Maint Court

THOMAS STREET

VIRGINIA ROW

SPITTLE SQUARE

LAMB STREET

Spittle Fields Market

West Str. East Str.

BROWNS

PELHAM LANE

CHURCH STREET

WHITE ROW

PRINCES STREET

BOOTH STREET

PATERNOSTER ROW

Church Street

CHURCH STREET

Christ Church

Spittle Fields Church Yard

Burying Ground

WHITE CHAPEL STREET

DORSET STREET

FASHION STREET

WHITE ROW

TENTER GROUND

WENTWORTH

WHITE CHAPEL STREET

White Chapel

Mary Church Yard

CHAPEL

Published by John Pine & John Tinney in October 1746 according to Act of Parliament

LORD LOVAT, GENTLEMAN ROGUE

IN the year our map was published the Earl of Kilmarnock and Lord Malmerino were beheaded on Tower Hill. Meanwhile a more widely-known Jacobite intriguer, 80-year-old Simon Fraser, Lord Lovat, lay in the Tower awaiting trial. His execution, in 1747, was the last performed in this country with an axe.

Because of Lovat's long life of adventurous roguery and treachery, a great crowd collected on the morning of April 9 to see him die. Over a thousand Guards, on foot and mounted, kept the masses back from the scaffold. A stand fell before the hour of the execution, causing many deaths in the crowd.

The grim old man, waiting to be brought to the scaffold, heard of this. "The more mischief the better sport," he remarked. From the scaffold a little later he surveyed the vast assembly and the soldiers. "Why," he asked, "should there be such a bustle about taking off an old head that cannot get up three steps without two men to support it ? "

Lovat was tall, very upright for his age, but made himself an odd figure by wearing a tremendous amount of clothing. " He has a large mouth and short nose, with eyes very much contracted and down-looking, a very small forehead almost all covered with a large periwig," says a writer of the period. " This gives him a grim aspect, but upon addressing anyone he puts on a smiling countenance." Hogarth sketched a famous portrait that bears out this description, at St. Albans, when Lovat was being brought to the Tower after capture in Scotland.

Simon, Lord Lovat, from Hogarth's original etching 1746

Lovat is also described as uniting " the peculiarities of a wild Highland chief with those of a cultivated gentleman," for he was a Master of Arts.

A wide, deep moat surrounded the Tower at this date : it was not drained until 1843. Entrances to the fortress were by drawbridges at the south-western angle ; and from the river over Traitor's Bridge under St. Thomas's Tower.

From the outline of the 800-year-old White Tower in the centre of the fortress it appears that the original entrance to the White Tower, an external stair, was still in being when our map was made. But the plan was probably copied from an earlier drawing. The stairway is thought to have been removed in Charles II's time, when some children's bones were found at the foot of it. They were identified, conjecturally, as the remains of Edward V and his brother, who disappeared mysteriously at the accession of Richard III.

The present Royal Mint occupies an area almost as extensive as the Tower itself. It replaced the Victualling Office of our map, the buildings of which later became tobacco warehouses.

Immediately east of the Tower, St. Katherine's Docks, opened in 1828, occupy about 24 acres, bounded by East Smithfield, Nightingale Lane, Burr Street, and St. Catherine's Way. They displaced the old Hospital of St. Katherine's by the Tower. It was a royal hospital, college, or free chapel, founded in 1148. It was removed to its present site in Regent's Park in 1825.

In clearing the ground for the docks, 1250 houses and 11,300 inhabitants also were displaced. The earth excavated filled reservoirs at Chelsea and Pimlico.

On the east side of Nightingale Lane is the west London Dock and Wapping Basin, excavated a few years earlier. Warehouses of both groups of docks were much damaged by the bombing raids of September 1940.

Rosemary Lane is now Royal Mint Street ; Cable Street has supplanted Knock Fergus, an Irish colony, somewhat disreputable : also spelled Knokvergence—it was an old name for Carrickfergus on Belfast Lough. Pennington Street marks the northern side of West London Dock ; and Red Maid Lane (now Redmead Lane) its southern border. Wapping Entrance is immediately west of Wapping Old Stairs.

Tower Bridge crosses the river to Bermondsey from Iron Gate Stairs to Horsleydown Old Stairs. Horsleydown Lane is Tower Bridge Lane ; Horsleydown Fair and New streets are now Tooley Street.

Bill Sykes's exciting and dramatic end, in *Oliver Twist*, occurred in Jacob's Island, the water-bound area of Jacob Street. Dickens's startling revelation of this grim district was of the period of 1850. He implied that thirty or forty years earlier it had been a thriving place.

The " island " no longer exists ; all traces of the ditches of evil-smelling mud at low tide were removed long ago. But our map helps one to realise the novelist's picture of Folly Ditch, into which Sykes thought to lower himself with a view to fighting his way out through the wild mob and the police.

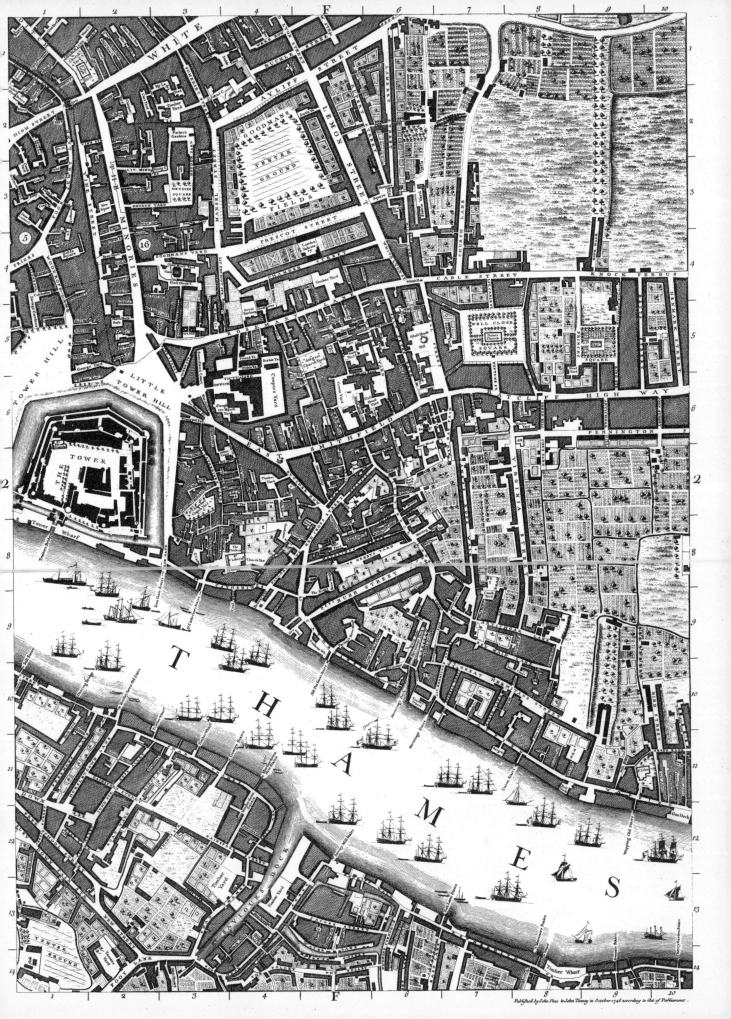

Published by John Pine & John Tinney in October 1746 according to Act of Parliament.

THE NECKINGER IN RURAL BERMONDSEY

SEVERAL Sections of our map present at a glance a great contrast between the London of two hundred years ago and the London we know. In no other Section is that contrast more marked than it is here.

This is a considerable portion of Bermondsey (except the left-hand bottom corner), and in 1746 it was a scene of open country, with tree-lined roads on which even the wayside inns were few and far between. On the whole of this Section only four are named : the Ship at one end of Blue Anchor Road, the Blue Anchor itself at the other ; the Bull and Butcher at the cross-roads between them ; and the Greyhound to the north of the turnpike in the Kent Road.

Around the Grange, once the great farm centre of the Abbey of Bermondsey, fields and market gardens are watered by numerous inlets derived from the Thames. This was low-lying country intersected by waterways, and it was probably marshland in early times. Despite the rural picture of our map, however, there are first signs of two important industries of the many that were soon to take possession, crowding this area with factories, workshops, and the inevitable small dwellings of the workers. Thus the Grange is already a centre of tanning, and in three places there are " walks " for the making of ropes.

Through the ditch on the east side of Jacob's Island flows the narrow tidal stream, or inlet, known as the Neckinger, seen in this Section along the north side of the road of the same name.

The word is a cant form of neckerchief, and suggests a winding waterway that almost ties itself in knots. The Neckinger was once navigable from the river to Bermondsey Abbey, and even on our map it runs down into Grange Walk as a ditch at the roadside, and there is a branch into the Grange.

Neckinger Road, continued west, is Abbey Street to-day, and Neckinger is the name of the road running south to the junction of Grange Road and Rope Maker's Walk. The latter two thoroughfares are now Spa Road. Grange Walk still exists, but half of it is called Horney Lane.

From the east end of Neckinger Road of our map, Jamaica Road now curves south and east to join the road unnamed that runs past the ends of Salisbury, Marygold, and Cherry Garden streets. In Cherry Garden Street, but just outside this Section, was the Jamaica House and Tea Gardens, which survived until 1888. Pepys visited Jamaica gardens one day in 1667, when " the girls did run for wages over the bowling green," and the diarist " with much pleasure, spent little."

Blue Anchor Road was named from the tavern at its eastern end on this Section ; the thoroughfare was renamed Southwark Park Road in 1878. The Blue Anchor was a popular sign of early times : in 1761 there were in London at least twenty-five alleys, courts, and yards so named.

From the turnpike in the Kent Road (Old Kent Road), the thoroughfare running north-east, and not named, was Upper Grange Road and is now Dunton Road ; and the first turning on the right, opposite the Greyhound, is Rolls Road, running south-west. The tree-lined hedge running parallel to it is now Lynton Road.

Thus the chief roads, all of them now fed by countless small streets, residential and commercial. However, it was the construction of what used to be called the Greenwich Railway, and later the South Eastern and Chatham Railway, traversing a region of market gardens through Spa Road station to London Bridge ; and, in an even greater measure, the branch line from New Cross (beyond the south-east corner of the Section) to Bricklayers' Arms goods station, which did so much to alter the map in this Section.

THE MANSION HOUSE

This building was begun in 1739 during the Mayoralty of Micajah Perry, and was appointed a Mansion House for the use of the Lord Mayor of the City of London. Sir Crisp Gascoigne, Lord Mayor in 1753, was the first to use it.

—*from an old engraving*

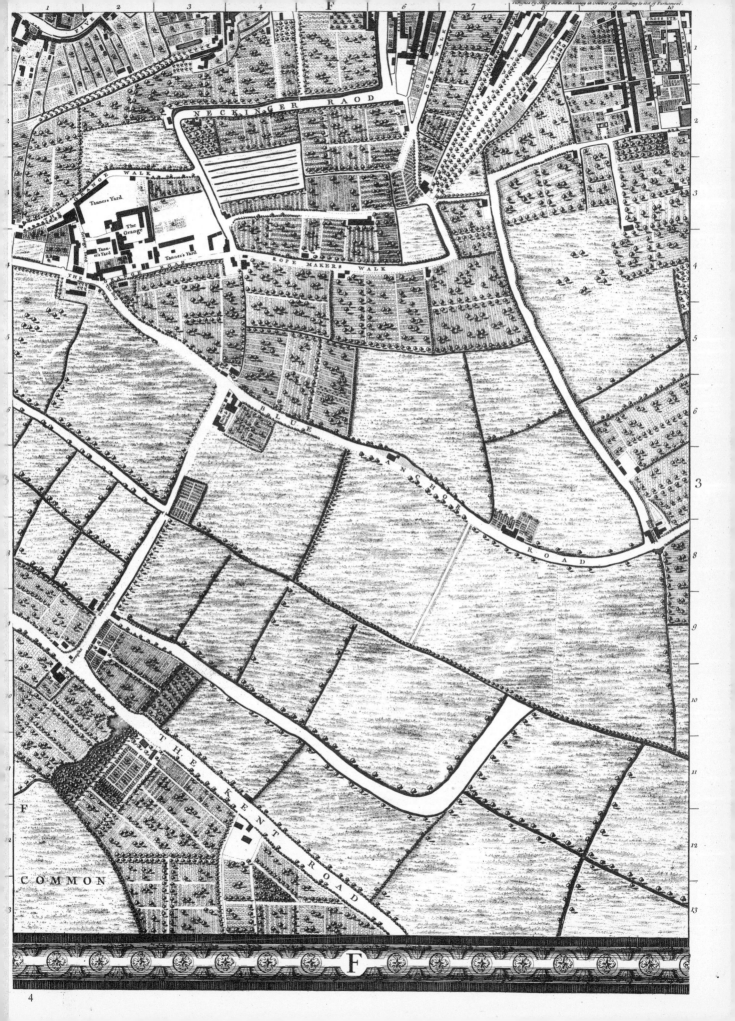

Publishd by John the 2 . 20th day in October 174 according to Act of Parliament.

CROSS STR.

FIVE

NECKINGER RAOD

ROPE WALK

ROPE WALK

Tanner's Yard

The Orange

Tanner's Yard

Tanner's Yard

THE

ROPE MAKERS' WALK

BLUE

ANCHOR

ROAD

THE KENT ROAD

F

COMMON

ROYAL CAVALCADE AT MILE END

BETHNAL GREEN is a small hamlet, and Mile End a little country town on our map.

South of the Watch House at Bethnal Green cross-roads is a large mansion which, in 1746, was a madhouse : it is so described, in letters difficult to decipher with a magnifying glass. From available evidence it may be identified as the mansion Pepys visited in June 1663 : " By coach to Bednall Green to Sir W. Rider's to dinner. A fine merry walk with the ladies alone after dinner in the garden : the greatest quantities of strawberries I ever saw, and good."

Tradition held at that time that the legendary Blind Beggar of Bethnal Green built this house. In fact, it is known that it was built for a tenant previous to Sir William Rider, namely, John Kirby, a wealthy Elizabethan.

It was a lunatic asylum for many years, but it must have been rebuilt between the date of our map and the time of its replacement by a block of modern dwellings.

Bethnal Green Museum, opened in 1872, occupies the space north of the Watch House. It was projected as a sort of poor relation of the Victoria and Albert Museum at South Kensington. No other district would accept the cast-off temporary iron structure of the latter when it was offered in 1865. It was unsightly and was called derisively the Brompton Boilers. A better-looking and more substantial building was made of it at Bethnal Green, where it was given brick walls and a broad frieze, under the so-called boiler roof.

There are references to Mile End—it is a mile from Aldgate—as a pleasant place, in the writings of Shakespeare, Beaumont and Fletcher, Thomas Heywood, Ben Jonson, and Pepys. It was a country resort for fresh air, cakes, and ale, in the diarist's time, and at the time of our map.

Sir Walter Raleigh stayed in the little town in 1596, and Captain James Cook lived in a house on the site of 88 Mile End Road in 1771–2.

Mile End Green is shown on our map as being near the turnpike. Other authorities place it farther east, in the right-hand turning, also called Mile End Old Town on our map, that is now Stepney Green. Wheatley identifies the latter as the meeting-place of the insurrectionists and Richard II in 1381.

The imposition in 1380 of a poll-tax on all over the age of fifteen, had provoked a popular uprising, directed chiefly against the gentry and landholders. " On the next morning all the men from Kent and Essex met at the said place called Mileende," says the City record of the insurrection. " There the King came to them from the Tower, accompanied by many knights and esquires, and citizens on horseback, the lady his mother following him also in a chariot. Where at the prayer of the infuriated rout, our Lord the King granted that they might take those who were traitors against him, and slay them, wheresoever they might be found."

Apparently the men of Essex went home, but the men of Kent, under Wat Tyler, went on to sack and burn in London. On the morrow the young King met them in Smithfield, when Wat Tyler was struck down by William Walworth, the Mayor, and later died.

Most of the roads in this Section are readily identified to-day. Near the top, the cross-country route from the George Inn beside the western border, is Bethnal Green Road ; continued eastward, along what is called Drift Way, it is Roman Road. Back Lane, continued down the wavy, tree-lined avenue, is the Globe Road of to-day.

From Bethnal Green, the road south to the turnpike in Mile End Old Town (i.e. Mile End Road) is Cambridge Road ; Red Cow Lane is now Cleveland Street.

At the west end, in this Section, of Mile End Road, is Whitechapel Mount. This was a huge, useless dump, originally a relic of trenches dug for the defence of London in the Civil War of 1642. It was added to by debris from the Great Fire of 1666, and by later accumulations of rubbish, until it was over 300 feet long, 182 feet wide, and was higher than London Hospital buildings beside it. The City Corporation dispersed it in 1801.

All traces of Ducking Pond Row have disappeared. Whitechapel Station on the district railway, and several great warehouses, occupy the site. Brady Street comes down what was Ducking Pond Lane.

Between the words OLD and TOWN are almshouses of the Skinners' Company and of Trinity House. Both are there still, but many of the little houses have been derelict since the Nazi raids, which wrought such widespread devastation among poor homes in areas on both sides of this thoroughfare.

Mile End Green and its continuations, Lady Leeks Grove and Walk, and Mile End Green Lane, are now Raven Row, Adelina Grove, and Redmans Road ; Mile End Town, running up north-east to the main road, is now Stepney Green.

The narrow path crossing the Section south of a bowling green, is Oxford Street, Stepney. There is a small piece of Commercial Road East in the left-hand bottom corner of the Section.

The main line of the L.N.E.R., Liverpool Street to Stratford, cuts across the Section immediately below the unnamed turning in Dog Row, and runs almost parallel with the Mile End Road. From Bethnal Green Junction, near the west border of the Section, there is a branch line running north to Cambridge Heath and Hackney Downs, and so to Enfield.

Kirby Castle, The Blind Beggar's House

The George

BETHNAL GREEN

Watch Ho.

RAG LANE

DOG ROW

RED COW LANE

DOG ROW

CAMEL ROW

MILE

MILE END OLD TOWN

MILE END OLD TOWN

MILE END OR

Ducking Pond

DUCKING POND ROW

MILE END OLD TOWN

Lady Leeks Walk

MILE END GREEN

Bowling
Green

MILE-END-GREEN-LANE

Chapel Mount

Published by John Pine & John John Tinney in October 1746 according to Act of Parliam.

OLD ENGLAND'S WOODEN WALLS

A FEATURE of our map is the great number of ships, so picturesquely drawn by the cartographers, moored or in sail on the river. Here in the Pool, and towards Limehouse Reach, they are nearly all deep-sea craft, with tall masts for a great spread of canvas.

They are appropriate to eighteenth-century Rotherhithe on the south bank and Wapping on the north, for as will be seen from the number of timber yards and wharves, and the boat builders' and shipwrights' premises along both shores, industry and trade here depended on ships, their construction and upkeep. There were mast and block makers, sail makers, anchor smiths, and chain makers, also ship chandlers and other traders connected with the provisioning and repair of the wooden walls of old England.

A fleet was fitted out at Rotherhithe in the reign of Edward III to the order of the Black Prince and John of Gaunt, and though the craft of shipbuilding left the Thames with the advent of iron and steel, barge-building has continued the tradition of this riverside industry down to the present day.

A far greater number of ships come and go on the broad waters of the Thames nowadays. The trade of the Port of London has developed great docks on either side of the tideway since our map was drawn. Here in Wapping are a part of the London Docks, and in Rotherhithe part of the Surrey Commercial Docks.

There is no satisfactory explanation of the name Redriff for Rotherhithe, a word compounded of *Redhra*, a mariner, in Saxon, and *hyth*, a haven. Both names appear on our map. Gay and Pepys call it Redriff, and it seems to have had that name as early as Edward I. Waterside Londoners still call it Redriff.

The ancient parish of St. Mary boasted some distinguished residents. Admiral Sir John Leake was born in Rotherhithe, and George Lillo, the dramatist, was living here in 1735. He wrote *The London Merchant, or the History of George Barnwell*, a soulful tragedy which for many years was acted before the pantomime on Boxing Night, as a useful lesson to London apprentices who might be tempted, as George Barnwell was, to rob their masters.

Jonathan Swift conceived Lemuel Gulliver as an inhabitant of Rotherhithe : and so real was this imaginary Gulliver to readers of his *Travels*, published in 1726, that many Rotherhithe folk swore that they had known him in person.

As St. Mary's Church, in red brick with Portland quoins, was built in 1714—on the site of a 400-year-old edifice—its graceful spire was a comparatively new landmark on the river. Christopher Jones, captain of the *Mayflower* which carried the Pilgrim Fathers to America, was buried in the old churchyard in 1621. His crew were Rotherhithe men, and it was to Rotherhithe the old ship was brought to be broken up. The burying ground of St. Mary's shown on our map has been taken over by the Borough Council, and now is a well-kept garden.

A stone's-throw from St. Mary's Church is the entrance to Rotherhithe Tunnel for road traffic, opened in 1908. It runs underground to the riverside at a point west of the Surrey Docks entrance, and under the river to King Edward VII Memorial Park, which occupies the area on our map between Bell Wharf Stairs and Shadwell Dock Stairs. The tunnel emerges above ground below Broad Street on the eastern border of the Section.

At a lower level, near its Rotherhithe mouth, is Rotherhithe Station on the New Cross—Shoreditch East London Railway. This is the old Thames Tunnel, a heroic pioneer effort of tunnel construction by Isambard Brunel, begun in 1825 but not completed until 1843. It crosses under the river to Wapping Station, near King Edward Stairs on our map, and runs due north, under East Dock, to Shadwell Station on the north side of Bluegate Field (now Cable Street).

Shadwell Basin occupies a large part of the area between New Gravel Lane and Griffin Street, now Glamis Street ; East Dock lies between New and Old Gravel Lane ; and running across the latter is Tobacco Dock, which joins London west dock.

By Pelican Stairs is a famous old waterside tavern, the Prospect of Whitby ; and just outside this Section, west of Wapping New Stairs, is another, the Town of Ramsgate. These two alone remain of thirty-six that were in Wapping High Street and Wapping Wall a hundred years ago, such as the Anchor and Hope, the North American Sailor, the Ship and Whale, and the Gun. Warehouses and industrial premises have completely changed the famous old waterfronts of Wapping and Rotherhithe.

Execution Dock recalls the custom of hanging pirates in chains here at the water's edge, and leaving their lifeless bodies to be flung to and fro by the tides. A pirate was hanged here as late as 1735 ; in 1816, Townsend, the celebrated Bow Street runner, told of two men " hanging down the river," but did not specify the place.

In Sun Tavern Fields, Shadwell, ropes and cables from six to twenty-three inches in girth were being made at the time of our map : Back Lane and Bluegate Field are now Cable Street to recall this industry. Ratcliffe Highway and Upper Shadwell are now joined as The Highway : formerly St. George Street, it used to be known as the Regent Street of seamen, who seldom got farther into London.

Of the unnamed roads in the upper part of this Section, none can be identified to-day ; Commercial Road, however, enters it near the letter G, and leaves it north of Stepney Causeway.

Thameside scene. *From an engraving*

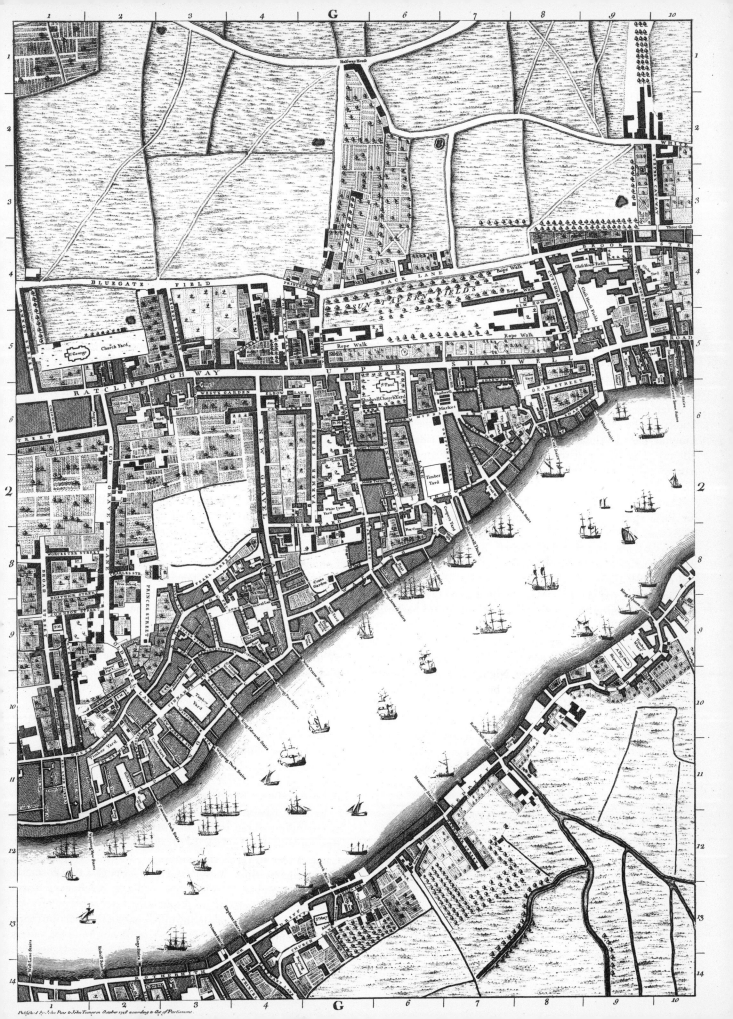

SIR JOHN BARNARD, GREAT COMMONER

THERE was not much of London in this Section of our map two hundred years ago. The area covered is south of the Rotherhithe river front, between Cherry Garden and Globe piers, and it consisted largely of market gardens, open fields, and a great expanse of marshland. To-day the whole of this Section is occupied by docks, warehouses, factories, business premises, houses, and two public parks.

Indicative of the great change that has come over this part of London is the fact that the railway stations of Rotherhithe, Surrey Docks, and South Bermondsey are in it now; and at the corner of Union Road (called New Paradise Street in our map) and Lower Road ("The Road to Deptford"), is the entrance to Rotherhithe Tunnel for vehicles and passengers, which runs under the Thames to Shadwell. Opened in 1908, it is a mile and a quarter long with its approaches.

In the top left-hand corner of our map is a series of little streets you can trace on a modern map. Most westerly is West Lane, which still bears that name. Its unnamed extension, winding down and out of the centre of the Section on its left-hand side, is now Southwark Park Road. In place of the wooded fields and market gardens it passed through in 1746 there is now a little maze of residential streets; but a large area of those fields on the right of the road, i.e. east of it, is Southwark Park.

"The Road to Deptford" on our map is now Lower Road. It skirts Southwark Park on its east side, and its continuation is Evelyn Street, leading to little Deptford Park. This falls within the elaborate panel whereon the publishers of our map inscribed their dutiful dedication.

The next named streets, Love Lane, continuing into Lucas Street, are now one as Cathay Street; beyond Love Lane is King Street, coming south from King's Stairs, and Queen Street. All lead into Paradise Street, called Old Paradise Street in our map. To the east of Queen Street is a very narrow street the incomplete name of which can be read through a magnifying-glass: Clark Orchard.

Some four hundred yards west of West Lane—just outside this Section—is Cherry Garden Street leading off the Pier: if you have ever stepped off a Thames steamer at this pier you must have wondered how such an uninspiring spot came by its pretty name. The fact that there was another orchard so near suggests that here was a place where Londoners might go "to see the cherry hung with snow" at Eastertide. Cherry Garden in the time of the Stuarts was a pleasant place of public resort, and Pepys, of course, was a visitor.

Next to Clark Orchard is Princess Street, leading into Back Lane; the latter is now St. Mary Street, and it joins

Sir John Barnard

New Paradise Street, now Union Road, near the entrance to Rotherhithe Tunnel. The much older Thames Tunnel, through which the East London Railway runs, comes out north of this Section, and Rotherhithe Station on that railway, below ground, is about the position of the letter G.

Southwark Park was so named because the market-garden land on which it was laid out in 1865–9, was then within the Parliamentary area of that borough. There had been a much earlier Southwark Park, the estate of Suffolk House in Henry VIII's time, a sumptuous mansion renamed Southwark Place when it came into King Henry's hands. This was near to St. George's Church, in Borough High Street, and between its site and the Southwark Park of to-day the whole of Bermondsey lies; so it would be more reasonable to name it Bermondsey Park. Its making cost the Metropolitan Board of Works £53,000, and its boating lake cost another £2000.

Quite a quarter of this Section, that is most of the marshland, is now taken up by some of the Surrey Commercial Docks: a portion of Albion Dock, the whole of Canada Dock, half of Quebec Dock, and a corner of Greenland Dock, are in it. The latter is the successor to Howland's Great Wet Dock, the story of which is told in Section H 3. As in the other groups of London docks, conspicuous targets for Hitler's bombs, there was much destruction during air attacks on London, of warehouses, refrigerating stores, and storage sheds. Facilities for the handling and storage of cargoes are being restored.

The dedication panel of John Pine and J. Tinney, the publishers of our map, is illuminated with cherubic figures pouring over the names of the City fathers, gold and wheat and produce symbolic of the City's far-flung overseas trade. The crowned central figure, representing the City itself, has placed its Cap of Liberty on the end of its staff.

Sir Richard Hoare, Knight, Lord Mayor in 1745, was the second son of Henry Hoare, banker, who purchased the estate of Stourhead, Wiltshire, from Lord Stourton, and settled there in 1720.

One of the Aldermen, Sir John Barnard of Dowgate Ward, represented the City in the House of Commons during 1722–1761. He was a wine merchant, also an authority on financial questions. During the panic of 1745, when public confidence in the Bank of England was declining, Barnard persuaded the leading City merchants to receive the Bank notes. For this and other services a movement was on foot, when our map was printing, to erect a statue of Barnard in the Royal Exchange. This was done in the following year.

Barnard was a type of honourable British merchant. He was often referred to by Pitt, Earl of Chatham, as "The Great Commoner." He had been Lord Mayor in 1737: in 1740 he published *A Present for an Apprentice; or a Sure Guide to gain both Esteem and an Estate, by a late Lord Mayor of London.*" This was a curious medley of Christianity and commerce, containing hints on all subjects, from buying a horse to selecting a nurse.

Map margins: 1 2 3 4 G 5 6 7 8 9 10

Published by John Pine & John Tinney in October 1746 according to Act of Parliament.

OLD PARADISE STREET · NEW PARADISE STREET · THE ROAD TO DEPTFORD

Cartouche dedication:

To the Rt. Honourable Sr. Rich. Hoare Knt.
LORD MAYOR, and Alderman of the Ward of Farringdon without, &
To the Rt. worshipful the Court of Aldermen of the City of London, viz:

Aldermen	Ward	Aldermen	Ward
Sr. Robt. Baylis Knt.	Bread-street 2	George Arnold Esqr.	Cheap 13
Sr. Edwd. Bellamy Knt.	Bridge without	William Benn Esqr.	Aldersgate 14
Sr. Jno. Thompson Knt.	Candlewick 3	Sr. Robt. Ladbroke Knt.	Castle Baynard 15
Sr. Jno. Barnard Knt.	Dowgate 4	Sr. William Calvert Knt.	Portsoken 16
Micajah Perry Esqr.	Aldgate 5	Sr. Saml. Pennant Knt.	Bishopsgate 17
Sr. Danl. Lambert Knt.	Tower 6	John Blachford Esqr.	Cripplegate 18
George Heathcote Esqr.	Wallbrook 7	Francis Cokayne Esqr.	Cornhill 19
Sr. Robt. Willimott Knt.	Lime-street 8	Tho. Winterbottom Esqr.	Billingsgate 20
Sr. Henry Marshall Knt.	Farringdn. with. 9	Robert Alsop Esqr.	Coleman-street 21
John Stracey Esqr. RECORDER;		Crisp Gascoyne Esqr.	Vintry 22
Sr. Geo. Champion Knt.	Bridge within 10	Edward Davies Esqr.	Queenhith 23
Sr. Joseph Hankey Knt.	Langborn 11	Edwd. Ironside Esqr.	Cordwainer 24
William Baker Esqr.	Bassishaw 12	Tho. Rawlinson Esqr.	Broad str. 25

Sr. Jno. Bosworth Knt. Chamberlain. Tho. Garrard Esqr. Common Serjant, & Miles Man Esqr. Town Clerk.

This Plan (in Gratitude for ye Assistance received from them in the Execution of it) is most humbly Inscribed by their most obedt. humbl. Servants, John Pine, & J. Tinney.

N.B. The Figures annexed to the Names of the Wards in the Dedication, refer to the Divisions of the Wards in the Plan.

G

A MERRY PEAL WHEN BANCROFT DIED

MOST of the main thoroughfare crossing this Section west to east is Mile End Road ; but at the word Essex, towards the east, Bow Road begins.

The Jews' Old Burying Ground, against the west border, is the first cemetery acquired by Portuguese Jews after their re-settlement in this country in the reign of Charles II. Two years after our map was made a hospital was opened on the Mile End Road frontage of this ground. Rebuilt in 1913, it is now Beth Holim, a home for aged Jews, and is 253 Mile End Road.

The £28,000 charitable bequest of a much-hated man, Francis Bancroft's Hospital, is the next building shown on the north side of Mile End Road. It was three large red-brick buildings, in the early Georgian style, upon the three sides of a wide sweep of lawn. Twenty-four old men lived here in comfort, thanks to the wealth left by Bancroft ; and 100 boys received their schooling there out of the same funds. As was customary in almshouses of the period, there was a pleasant little chapel as a centre-piece. The whole made a charming picture at the time of our map—quite a contrast to the scene, twenty-two years earlier, at Bancroft's funeral.

Francis Bancroft, grandson of a notable Archbishop of Canterbury, was an officer of the Lord Mayor's Court. In these days he would have had a salary and no perquisites. But it is recorded of Bancroft that " he acquired his fortune by harsh acts of justice in his capacity as a City officer—by unnecessary informations and arbitrary summonses." Perhaps he had a stern sense of righteousness, but it would appear that he used it to line his pocket richly. And, " so unpopular was he," says Wheatley, " that the mob hustled the bearers of his coffin, and the church bells rang out a merry peal at his funeral."

He was strange, too, in that he endowed an extraordinary tomb in St. Helen's, Bishopsgate, for himself in his lifetime, and this is how it was described in 1773 : " He is embalmed in a chest made with a lid, having a pair of hinges without any fastening, and a piece of square glass in the lid just above his face. It is a very plain monument and has a door for the sexton to go in and clear it from dust and cobwebs."

He directed that the Wardens and Court of Assistants of the Drapers' Company were to pay an official visit on stated occasions, and lift the lid to inspect what was left of Francis Bancroft.

Of course he never saw the almshouses, the chapel, the school, and the cool green lawn : they remained to perpetuate his name more worthily until 1884. The almshouses were abolished then, and the school was transferred to Woodford Green, Essex. And out of the foundation of the bequest of this unusual man, his trustees, the Drapers' Company, have created the great public school of Bancroft's, in splendid premises on ten acres of ground in Epping Forest, with 16 acres of playing fields besides. There are still 100 boarders, but 300 day scholars also.

Bancroft's five-acre site in Mile End Road was bought by the Beaumont Trust, and the People's Palace and another great educational institution, Queen Mary College, University of London, have grown upon it.

The Jews' New Burying Ground, no longer new, still exists beside Queen Mary College, its tombstones all lying flat in accordance with Jewish custom. The road running south out of Mile End Road is Burdett Road. Foot Path to Bow is Solebay Street, leading to Cemetery Row and Tower Hamlets Cemetery. At Rhode's Well is a bridge over the Regent's Canal, this extension to the Thames being opened in 1820. The canal enters this Section in the north-west corner and flows under Mile End Road east of the Jews' New Burying Ground.

The road south from Rhode's Well is Rhodeswell Road ; the road running west from the well is Ben Jonson's Road ; and the road west of Stepney Church Yard leading to the Mercer's Almshouses (still there, but rebuilt, and reduced in number during the air raids) is Stepney High Street. A large part of the churchyard is now a public garden kept by the London County Council.

St. Dunstan's and All Saints', Stepney, known as the Church of the High Seas from the ancient custom of registering there any child baptised on board a ship flying the British flag, is of early fourteenth-century origin, but has been much rebuilt. A monument in the church to Dame Rebecca Berry, widow of Sir John Berry who died in 1696, bears his coat-of-arms. It includes a fish and an annulet, or ring, and this gave rise to the local tradition that Dame Berry was the heroine of the ballad called " The Cruel Knight, or fortunate Farmer's Daughter."

But this was an Arabian Nights tale. Nevertheless it is still told in Stepney how the Knight intended to drown the Farmer's Daughter, but relented. Throwing a ring into the sea, he bid her avoid him on pain of death unless she could produce to him that same ring. Eventually she chanced to find it in a fish she cut open, brought it to the Knight, who thereupon married her.

The flag of Admiral of the Fleet, Lord Tovey, who on the battleship King George V conducted the chase and action which resulted in the sinking of the Nazi battleship *Bismarck* in 1940, hangs in St. Dunstan's church.

St. Dunstan's, Stepney

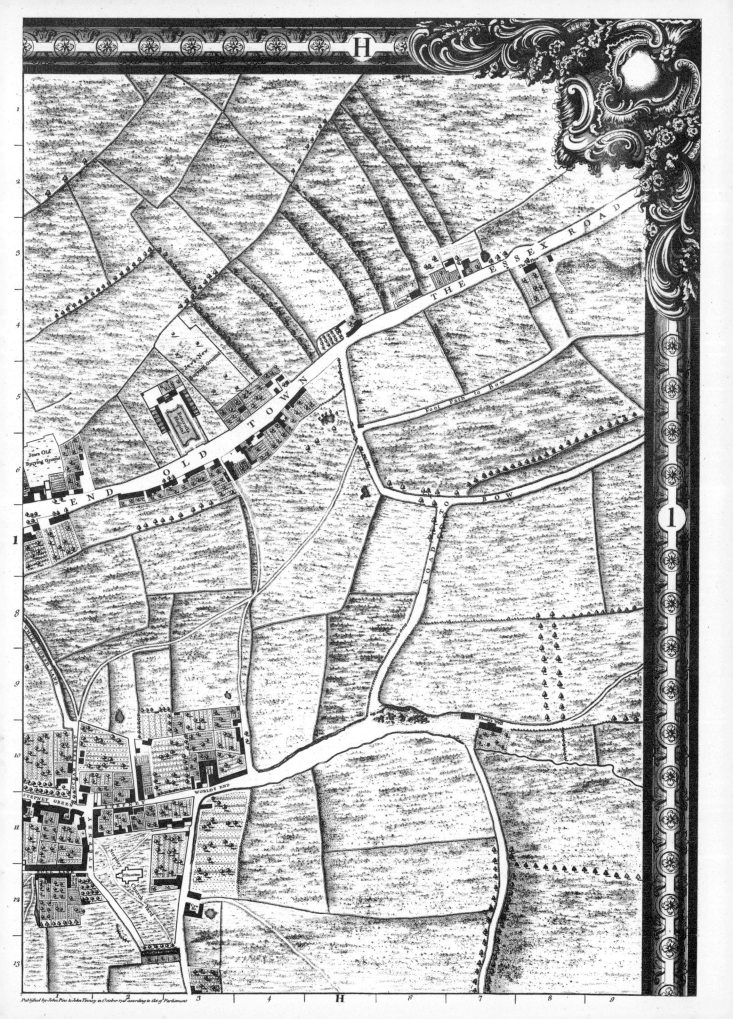

THE ESSEX ROAD

Foot Path to Bow

MILE END OLD TOWN

Jews New Burying Ground

Jews Old Burying Ground

ROAD TO BOW

Rhodes Well

WORLDS END

STEPNEY GREEN

STEPNEY

Dunstan

1

LIMEHOUSE HOLE AND ROTHERHITHE

NORTH of the river in this Section we are in Stepney and Limehouse. White Horse Lane, coming in from Whitechapel, now joins Rose Lane, and the whole is Commercial Road to the church of St. Anne, Limehouse. Here East India Dock and West India Dock roads begin, continuing beyond the eastern border of the map.

Other main thoroughfares north of the river, namely, White Horse Street, on the west side of the Section; Sermon (now called Salmon) Lane; and Three Colt Street in the east, survive to-day, with the same names.

Three Colt Street leads down into the area formerly known as Limehouse Hole; also to Limehouse Entrance—Limekiln Dock on our map—the passage from the river into West India Dock.

Charles Dickens in 1864, and Thomas Burke prior to 1917, wrote well-remembered books with Limehouse backgrounds. Neither writer would find now the streets and alleys, nor yet the types of men and women, that gave them their material. Still less would the waterside workers of two hundred years ago recognise to-day the scenes of their labours shown on our map.

Dickens's novel, *Our Mutual Friend*, gives us a glimpse, however, that was probably true enough of the Limehouse of 1746. Rogue Riderhood "dwelt deep and dark in Limehouse Hole, amongst the riggers, and the mast, oar and block makers, and the boat builders and the sail-lofts, as in a kind of ship's hold stored full of waterside characters. . . . The Hole, albeit in a general way not over nice in its choice of company, was rather shy in reference to the honour of cultivating the Rogue's acquaintance."

Monster warehouses of the wharfinger companies, some gutted during air attacks on the docks but others still operating, dominate the riverside now. And behind the waterfront are great blocks of modern L.C.C. dwellings, well-ordered giant beehive homes. The remaining wretched hovels formerly common to Limehouse were bombed out of existence by Hitler, leaving patches for a grass and weed-grown wilderness.

Limehouse Causeway, once exciting as the haunt of Chinese, Japanese, Lascar, and Maltese seamen, has practically disappeared. You must cross West India Dock Road, Poplar, just beyond the eastern border of our map, to Pennyfields, to find the few small, mysterious-looking tenements and restaurants, Chinese characters painted over their doors, that are the little Chinatown of to-day.

Narrow Street, along the Limehouse river front, is still narrow. It has an unwholesome air around a riverside depot for refuse, but there are one or two curious old boat-building shops over the water's edge, each with its own tiny dock for launching small craft. They survive from the period of our map.

On the opposite side of this street is the electricity generating station of Stepney Borough Council, a modern contrast to this centuries-old craft of boat-building. Its tremendous brick-built chimney, 345 feet high, the tallest in London, was completed in 1937, and is a landmark more conspicuous even than the lofty tower of St. Anne's Church at the top of Three Colt Street.

St. Anne's was built by Wren's pupil, Nicholas Hawksmoor, in 1712-24. Its tower, with four angular turrets and a more lofty one in the centre, is original and picturesque, and has thus been easily identified for a couple of centuries by ships coming up the river. It was dedicated to St. Anne as a compliment to the Queen. The churchyard is still spacious.

Into the north part of this Section two artificial waterways have been brought. Limehouse Cut, a canal functioning since about 1770, navigable by barges from the River Lea, enters the Section in the north-east corner and, passing under Commercial Road west of St. Anne's Church, locks into the Thames at what on our map is called Limehouse Bridge Dock.

A few yards to the west is Regent's Canal Entrance, leading to an 11-acre dock that deals mostly with seaborne coal. Regent's Canal enters the Section at the top, east of the letter H, passes under Salmon Lane, and enters the dock under Commercial Road in the middle of the Section. This stretch of Regent's Canal was completed in 1820.

South and west of the river is a part of Rotherhithe, occupied almost entirely by the Surrey Commercial Docks. They extend west and south into Section H 3, cover more than 381 acres, have a water area of 134 acres, and nearly 9 miles of quays.

Jamaica, Lavender, Queen, and Trinity Streets of our map, are now all one in Rotherhithe Street, a thoroughfare of riverside commerce and big modern blocks of dwellings. The name Cuckold's Point on the bend of the river survives as a river mark to-day: it was formerly marked by a tall pole with a pair of horns on the top.

Cuckold is a derisive term for a man whose wife is false to him. It arose here out of an impossible legend concerning a miller at Charlton. He discovered his wife in the arms of King John, who had been hunting in the district. As recompense for the wrong done to him, the King gave the miller all the strip of land he could see, on the facetious condition that he walked over this land once a year with a pair of buck's horns on his head. The legend claims that the miller saw as far as Rotherhithe, more than three miles distant as the crow flies. To walk direct to Rotherhithe shore the miller would have had to cross the river three times: but the silly story persisted through the ages.

The Pageants, also on the bend of the river on our map, survives in Pageant Stairs and Pageant Wharf. One can only guess that some forgotten river pageant was assembled or prepared at this point long ago, for there is no record of the derivation.

No one seems to know, either, how the Condemn'd Hole got its name. Originally it was a depot for flotsam collected on the river, a sort of pound. In more recent times it has been known as the Burning Ground, because tobacco condemned by the Customs and Excise department of the Inland Revenue was burned there. It is now a waterguard station of the Customs preventive staff.

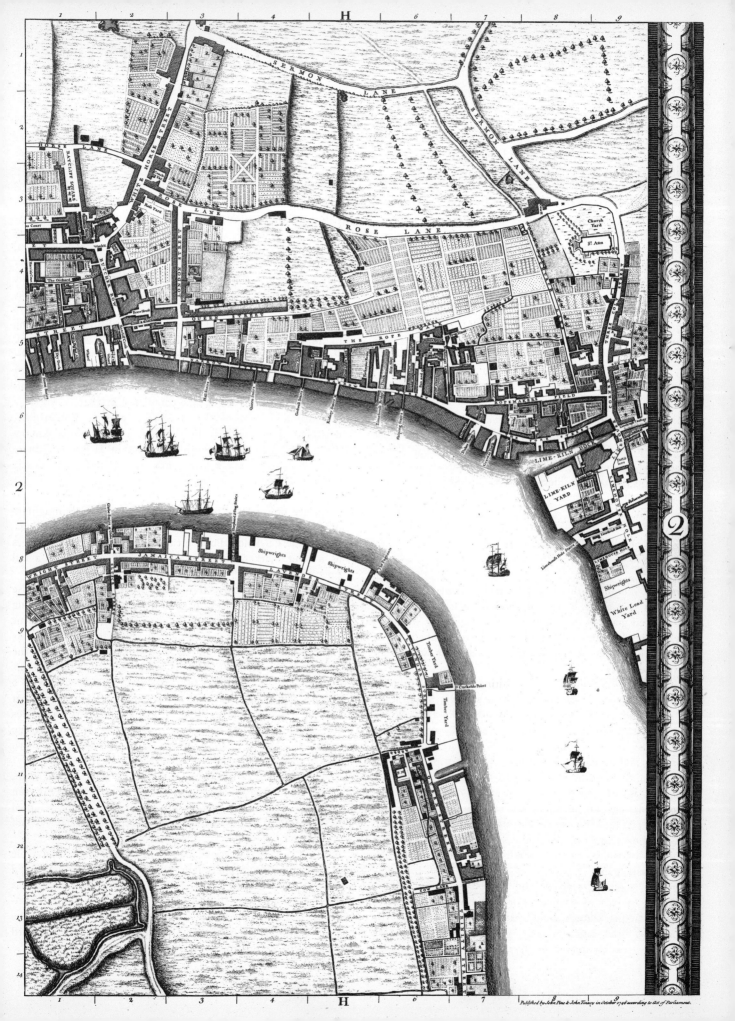

A DUKE AND TWO ASTUTE WIDOWS

SURREY COMMERCIAL DOCKS, extending south from Rotherhithe Street in Section H 2 almost to the Royal Victualling Yard, are an amalgamation of enterprises of the early nineteenth century, taken over in 1908 with all the other great London docks by the Port of London Authority. The nucleus of the system was the famous Howland Great Wet Dock, shown on our map as Upper Wet Dock.

This was the first wet dock ever constructed, and there is a curious story behind its conception. A duke and two astute widows were responsible for what in its time was a pioneer venture—the provision of a ten-acre stretch of still water, locked against the tide, on which 120 merchant ships could lie always afloat.

Its originators were Mrs. Elizabeth Howland, of Streatham, daughter of Sir Josiah Child, dictator chairman of the East India Company, and widow of a considerable landowner; the fifth Earl, later first Duke, of Bedford; and Lady Rachael Wriothesley Russell, widow of the Earl of Bedford's son, William Lord Russell, executed as a Rye House plotter in 1683.

The association of the Earl and the Howlands appears to have begun in 1681, when a marriage was arranged between Wriothesley, the infant son of Lady Russell (and the Earl's grandson), and Elizabeth, infant daughter of Mrs. Howland. It was an alliance to be between two wealthy, land-owning families; the Howlands owned the Rotherhithe land and other estates. Note the sequence of events which followed. The project for the dock was set out in a Bill read in the House of Lords in February 1695. It received the Royal Assent in April 1695, and the marriage of the children took place in May 1695, when the boy was fourteen and a half and the girl about a year younger.

In June 1695, the Earl, by this time Duke of Bedford, was created Baron Howland of Streatham in consequence of the marriage of his grandson and heir: clearly the barony was arranged on behalf of the boy-husband, heir not only to the Dukedom but to the Howland estates of his mother-in-law, now a widow.

After the marriage, Wriothesley and Elizabeth, now Marquis and Marchioness of Tavistock, met only at intervals for some years; but the Duke and Mrs. Howland saw a great deal of each other. She had a lot of money invested in the East India Company, and the Duke took up shares in the Company's ships, partly for dividends, but also to import goods for himself. Some fine pieces of oriental china

for Woburn and Bedford House came to the Howland Dock.

At its west end there was " a noble dwelling-house " belonging to the Duke : there is a drawing of this miniature mansion, made in 1796, on which it is recorded that " J. Wells Esq. bought it of the old Duke of Bedford who formerly resided there."

Sir Joseph Broodbank, in *History of the Port of London*, says, " it is exceedingly doubtful whether the discharge and loading of ships would have been permitted at the time of the construction of the dock, having regard to the unwillingness of the legal quays to suffer any infraction of their privileges." The Duke's house on the dock, however, could have been very convenient for private cargo.

John Wells, a Rotherhithe shipwright, leased the river front where there were two small dry docks and two launching slipways, and here were constructed the *Tavistock* and the *Streatham* in the Duke's lifetime. Both passed to the East India Company. Dying in 1700, the old Duke missed seeing the *Streatham* sail down the Thames on her first voyage that year.

Tavistock and *Streatham* were using the dock at the time of our map ; on April 5, 1755, Captain Clive and his lady were passengers in *Streatham* to India, sailing from Rotherhithe.

As for the dock, it is still in operation as the Greenland Dock, but is now much larger. Documents in the archives of the Russell family suggest that John Wells, the shipwright, designed the Howland Dock ; he and William Ogborne, house carpenter of Stepney, did all the timber work of dock and wharves, and there were contractors for the excavations. All their work had to be completed by September 29, 1697.

But there must have been more to it than a shipwright could achieve, and it is likely that two engineers, George Sorocold, who in 1702 improved the waterworks machinery at London Bridge ; and Thomas Steers, pioneer in the science of dock construction, provided the brains of the scheme. Steers later built the first Liverpool dock, a more difficult proposition.

Rogues Lane of our map is now Redriff Street and Redriff Lane ; Little Rogues Lane is Plough Road, continuing to the river below Mill Pond. This, with Lower Wet Dock, is now South Dock. Running south-east from The Artichoak is Evelyn Street, named after the diarist whose residence, Sayes Court, was situated just off our map.

Victualling Office Warehouses, established for the Navy a year before our map was made, are now the Royal Victualling Yard. The King's Yard was the famous Deptford dockyard created by Henry VIII, covering 36 acres. Many of the " wooden walls " of old England were built here. Queen Elizabeth, visiting the *Golden Hind* in 1581, knighted Frances Drake at Deptford.

The dockyard was in use until 1869. It has since been successively the Foreign Cattle Market and an Army stores depot.

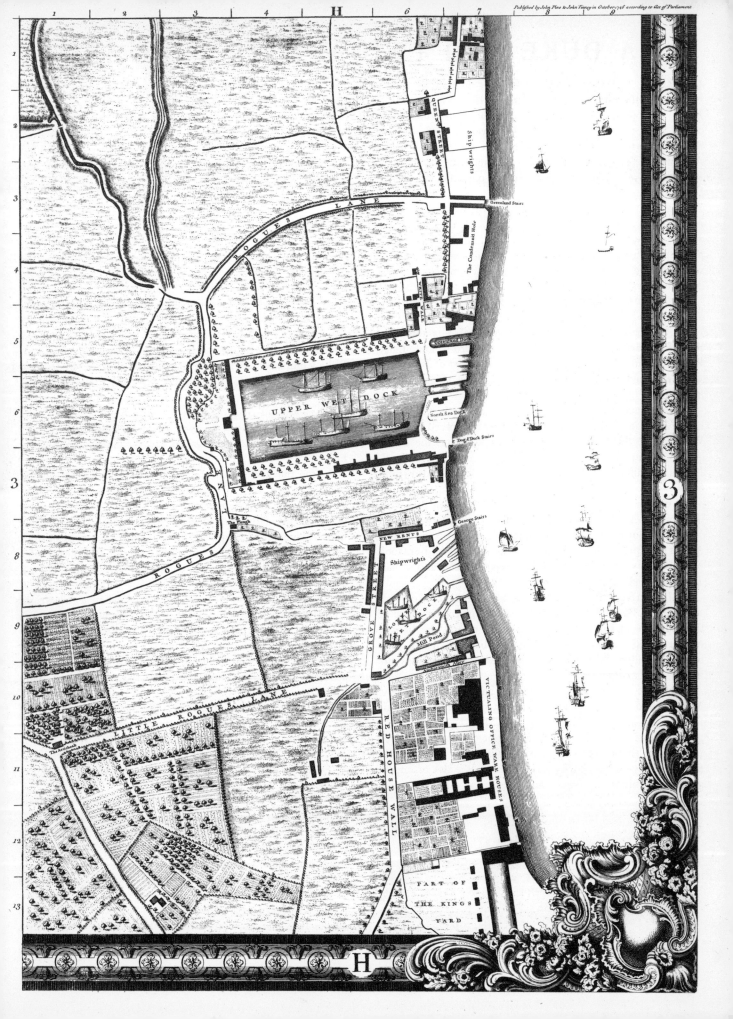

Published by John Pine & John Tinney in October 1746 according to Act of Parliament

1 2 3 4 H 6 7 8 9

QUEEN STREET

Shipwrights

Greenland Stairs

The Condemned Hole

Greenland Dock

UPPER WET DOCK

South Sea Dock

Dog & Duck Stairs

George Stairs

The Plough

NEW RENTS

Shipwrights

ROGUES LANE

GROVE STREET

Mill Pond

VICTUALING OFFICE WARE HOUSES

RED HOUSE WALL

LITTLE ROGUES LANE

PART OF THE KINGS YARD

3

H

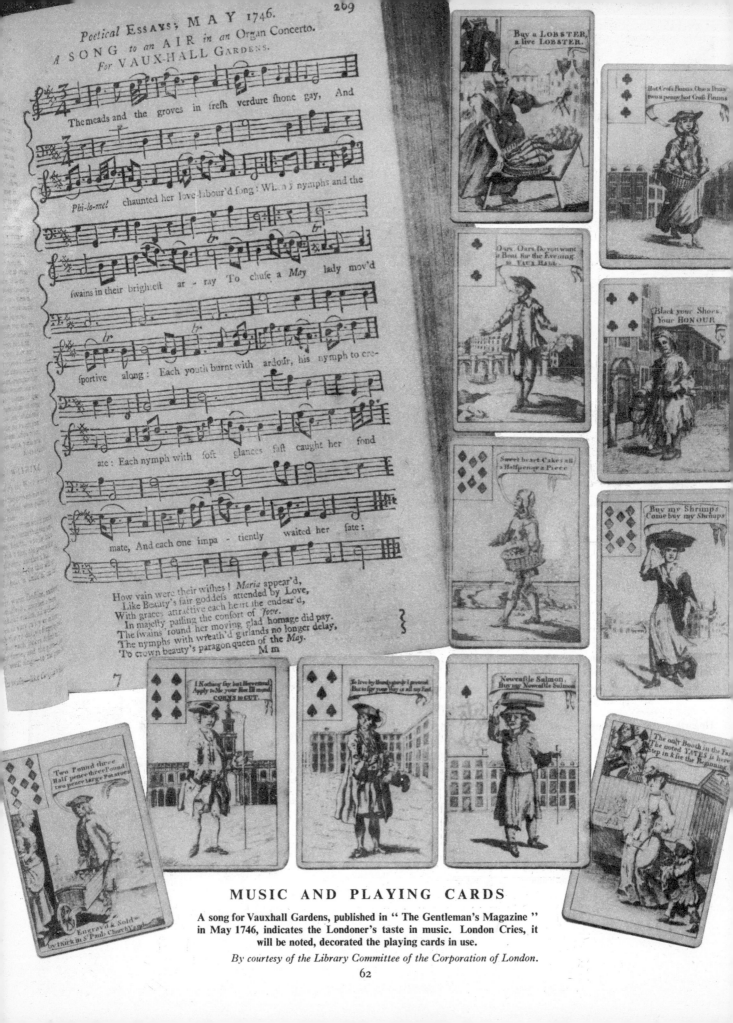

MUSIC AND PLAYING CARDS

A song for Vauxhall Gardens, published in " The Gentleman's Magazine "
in May 1746, indicates the Londoner's taste in music. London Cries, it
will be noted, decorated the playing cards in use.

By courtesy of the Library Committee of the Corporation of London.

"March of the Guards towards Scotland
in the year 1745," commonly called
"March to Finchley," was engraved
about 1750. It depicts the disorders of
a rear-guard after the departure of the
regiment. The main body are marching
away on the horizon to the camp at
Finchley, where an army was then
assembling. The rear-guard, left at
Tottenham Court turnpike, are having
difficulty in dislodging themselves from
the twin attractions of the fair sex and
fiery potations.

Hogarth put up the original painting to
lottery, i.e. he raffled it ; purchasers of
7s. 6d. tickets received a print. After
2000 had been disposed of the cost of
prints rose to half a guinea. Hogarth
gave all unsold tickets to the Foundling
Hospital, and one of these secured the
original painting.

Hogarth, who was apprenticed to a
silver engraver, himself executed the
design of the raffle ticket, with its trophy
of military weapons, tools, and musical
instruments.

By courtesy of M. R. Holmes, F.S.A.

63

THE GATES OF LONDON

Ald Gate.

Moor Gate.

REMINDERS that London grew out of a walled city that could only be entered in earliest times by gates in its walls, were still to be seen at the time of our map. These gates remained until 1760–2, when all were demolished as obstructions.

There is no exact age record of three of the oldest, Ludgate, Aldersgate and Aldgate, though popular tradition holds that Ludgate was built in 66 B.C. by King Lud, who was said to have built the City's first walls. Bishopsgate was built in 685; Cripplegate existed before the

Bishops Gate.

Cripple Gate.

Alders Gate.

New Gate.

Lud Gate.

Temple Barr.

Illustrations by courtesy of the Library Committee of the Corporation of London.

Conquest, according to Stow; Moorgate's date is 1415; Newgate's, early in the 12th century. Each of these seven gates had been rebuilt from time to time.

Temple Bar, constructed from Wren's design in 1670 to replace a timber house that had a narrow gateway beneath it, was not a gate in the City wall, but a limit on the west of the City liberties. It took the place of posts, rails and chains, termed bars, also put up at Smithfield, Whitechapel and Holborn.

MADE AND PRINTED IN GREAT BRITAIN BY MORRISON AND GIBB LTD., LONDON AND EDINBURGH
PUBLISHED BY ASSOCIATED NEWSPAPERS LTD., LONDON, E.C.4